When You Pray

Words for Searching Your Soul in Prayer

Also by Michael K. Washington

Hope: Meditations Before, During, and After Advent

Endure: Meditations for Lent and Other Seasons of Prayer

Follow: Walking With Jesus One Week at a Time

The section "Prayers for Waiting" are all taken and adapted from my book, *Endure: Meditations for Lent and Other Seasons of Prayer.*

Cover Photo by Anatoliy Gromov on Unsplash.

Author Photo by Jantzen Loza Photography.

ISBN: 978-0-9980507-5-1

My website: www.michaelwashington.org

For New Community

Contents

Gratitude.. 13

An Explanation 14

Prayers For Openings 13

Open.. 14

Closing.. 16

Listening 19

Wisdom Of Words.. 21

Unhelpful Words... 24

When My Spirit Closes 27

Early Glimpses 30

Deepening The Quiet... 32

In The Dark 34

Indwelling 37

Come 39

PRAYERS FOR DISCERNMENT.......................... 41

Those Fears Are Real.. 42

Imagining A Beginning.. 44

Renewed Vision 46

What's Next?... 48

Being A Person Of Faith....................................... 51

Trusting You.. 54

All Goes Quiet 56

This Choice 58

Teach Us To Pray 60

Our Collective Future 62

Surrendering All 64

Prayers For Love.. 66

Being In Love 67

Dealing With Hate 69

On The Path Of Love 71

Identity As Love 73

So Loved The World.. 75

Pictures 77

Moments 79

Nourishing Love 81

Imitating Love.. 83

Heartbreak 85

My Vision 87

Prayers For Waiting... 89

Help Me 90

Today.. 93

Perfect Love... 96

Waiting For Healing... 98

Praying Into Me 100

Tears 102

Unconditional 104

What I Need To Trust 106

Give 108

Good News 111

Grow My Soul.. 113

Prayers For Worship 115

You.. 116

Worth 118

When I'm Convinced 120

Who You Are... 122

View More 124

If You Stopped 126

John 11 Breath Prayers... 128

Select Images Of God... 130

Threaten All I Worship 133

Greatness 135

First 137

Prayers For Peace... 140

Be Peace.. 141

Within My Soul 143

New Images 145

Keep My Soul 147

Times Of Violence 149

Traumas 151

When I Sit 153

Breathing 155

Middles 157

Circles Of God's Company 160

Prayers For Suffering 162

Changing... 163

The Presence... 165

Anguish.. 167

This Present Time 169

Jesus... 171

Shame 173

Sickness.. 175

Patient Care.. 177

Crossing, Committing, And Carrying 179

Unseen Futures 181

Slow Repentance Of Slow Sin 183

Prayers For Creativity... 186

The Chaos.. 187

Waiting For You 189

When 191

Making Music.. 193

Wondering Through The Maze 195

Ideas 198

Sifting Through Things 200

Outpouring 202

My Clenched Hands 204

One Sanctuary.. 206

Unspeakable... 208

Give Me Joy 210

Communion With God 212

Things I Wonder About 214

Memory 216

A Way Opening 218

Prayers For Doubt 220

Unknowing 221

Sweet Holy Spirit 223

In Your Hands 225

My Eyes 227

My Futures 229

My Unwritten Words 231

Wide Invitations... 233

Fists And Fingers 235

Join Me 237

Skills Of Gratitude 239

Risk 241

Enduring The Broadness 243

Prayers For Grief 245

Noticing Losses 246

Daddy 248

Acquainted With Grief 250

Rooms For My Grief 252

Pressing Me Away 254

Questions 256

Tears 258

Lynching 260

Shedding And Gaining 262

On A Hill 264

Trust 266

Prayers For Others 268

Prayers Of The People 269

What I Can't Face 271

Your Job 273

Loved 275

For A Friend Who's Hospitalized 277

For A Friend Looking For Work 279

For Students And Teachers Beginning 281

A Friend Struggling With Suicidal Thoughts 284

For A Friend Readying For Marriage.. 286

After You Pray 288

Gratitude

Thank you, Linda Swanson, for your specific ways of reading these prayers as prayers and giving me feedback, including telling me what these words were and what they weren't. Also, thank you, Aja Carr-Favors, for the original prompt to do these, a moment you've probably forgotten. Finally, thank you, New Community Covenant Church for being a community that has taught me many things before, around, under, and in these prayers.

An Explanation

This is a book with brief daily invitations to open your soul. I'm inviting you into speaking with God through the practice of centering prayer. In other words, this particular way of praying is about getting you into a way of opening your soul and eventually listening, both to your soul and to God.

I think of prayer as a space where God listens to us. Of course, prayer is also a space where we listen to God. My definition of prayer is broad. It means that prayer is speech that we want God to hear. It may or may not begin with a title. We may use a formula; we may not. Prayer is speech that we need God to hear. On the other hand, in prayer, God also says things, communicates things that we need to hear. In listening we are changed. Have you ever listened to your own prayers? Have you ever sensed God's response to your prayerful words? Listening will change you. What is centering prayer and how might it fit in your prayer life?

Centering prayer is a method of praying that involves using words, images, and phrases in order to center yourself with God. To center yourself with God means to place yourself with God, to imagine yourself sitting with God, to see yourself circling around the Presence of God who actively encircles you. When using centering prayer, you sit with God, you settle with God, and you circle with God. You generally will use a word, symbol, phrase or prayer to draw you into the sitting, settling, and circling.

That said, in praying with centering prayer, you draw upon a phrase, for instance, to center down and to focus upon God by using that phrase. The phrase helps you attend to God. The phrase helps you excuse other words, phrases, and thoughts so that you can *be* in the presence of God. The phrase or image or entire prayer helps you sit with God. In that way, a prayer can be your guide. A sentence can be your tool. One word can be your entry into prayerfulness. The point is for you to keep company with God, to attend to God.

The goal of centering prayer is listening in God's presence. The hope of the prayer practice is the act of keeping company with God. The hope is to become less distracted by things taking away from the love of God by opening yourself to friendship with God. That means that the end is not the silence (or the listening) but the One with whom you're silent. Centering prayer is an effort in that direction. You can't control God's Presence—and whether you'll sense that Presence—but you can attend faithfully to silencing what you can. That's where centering comes in.

Here are a few practical guidelines for entering into this prayer practice:

1. Choose a time and place where you can pray quietly for up to 20 minutes.
2. Use the words, lines, or complete prayers in the offerings in the book.
3. Acknowledge your distractions and that they're real.
4. Excuse your distractions and let them know you'll return to them.
5. Gently engage the practice in God's presence.

These prayers intend to be broken up when needed or read as slowly as possible. You may stay with a phrase or a line. I encourage you to do so because it'll lengthen you use of the prayers. Staying with a phrase or a line will also help you practice centering prayer. Centering is done best when few words are your guides or when one image is your anchor. In that way, each prayer is full of centering *prayers*. That said, you may use the full prayer throughout a day. You'll notice that I don't offer any titular openings for God. Though I'm always writing as a Christian, my biblical tradition has so many titles and addresses for God and my tradition only and always assumes God's *presentness* that I simply continue in the assumption of God's already listening acts when I start praying. Beyond that, my intention is to offer you multiple routes into the quiet holiness, the quiet wholeness, in God's nearness.

To note one matter of word choice, where I have used a single gendered pronoun, it's after great work to not do that. I've tried to write prayers that anyone, female or male, can pick up and use. I am also aware in my praying and in my writing that those two binaries are, to different degrees, not comfortable for people. Where I have chosen to refer to a gendered person, I've used a masculine pronoun because of my own gender. I'm praying these prayers before you. At times, I get around this by using a female pronoun. I choose both to try to be balanced. I point it out here because I'm considering your reading experience while praying. The last intention is for you not to pray with these words. Do what helps you use my words.

Finally, if these prayers feel like good hosts to you, experiment with your own prayers. Write them. Or, simply, utter them. Aren't the best prayers those truths that emerge from long life lived with God? I've found the guides you'll see quotes from to be extremely helpful in my own prayers. I commend these folks to you. Their collections of spiritual wisdom will be a good use to you if you find my prayers helpful. I think of these folks as kin, so join the family of these witnesses. We'll keep praying together, deepening in our quiet with God together.

Michael
In the season after Pentecost, 2017

PRAYERS FOR OPENINGS

"We are most alive when we are brought face to face with the response of the deepest thing in us to the deepest thing in life…This we know in prayer at its best and highest. Then we pass through all the external aspects of our situation and need, then the walls of our pretensions are swept away and we are literally catapulted out of the narrow walls that shut us in."

Howard Thurman, *The Inward Journey*, 19-20

OPEN

Before You Pray

- Choose a time to pray.

- Choose a place to pray.

- Use the words, lines, or complete prayers in the offerings in the book.

- Acknowledge your distractions and that they're real.

- Excuse your distractions and let them know you'll return to them.

- Gently engage the practice in God's presence.

When You Pray

It's easier to be closed, easier to sit in the safety of noise.

My days are filled with noise.

My days are filled with steady streams of stuff that keeps me from paying attention to you.

As I try to come to you, open me to the possibility of more.

Open me to the world that's waiting.

Open me to connection that can come between us as I wait in a wordless moment.

I'm not sure about being open.

I've learned that closing down brings good, less stress, and less conflict.

I've been convinced to stay away from the quiet of this type of praying.

If I'll open, it'll have to start with what you know.

After You Pray

- Sit and listen.

- Write what you hear, sense, see.

- Create something.

- Keep praying.

- Write your own prayer.

CLOSING

Before You Pray

- Choose a time to pray.

- Choose a place to pray.

- Use the words, lines, or complete prayers in the offerings in the book.

- Acknowledge your distractions and that they're real.

- Excuse your distractions and let them know you'll return to them.

- Gently engage the practice in God's presence.

When You Pray

Close the old doors, the rickety doors keeping me from hearing.

They are the doors to the rooms that tell me listening is worthless.

They are the doors to the places that convinced me to keep talking.

They are the doors to the homes that harmed my soul.

Close the old rooms, the ones that hemmed me into smallness and decreasing life.

Diminish the places that my heart once held in regard.

Turn me away from the homes that were all I knew.

Close the old places that sullied my spirit and made me lose my real self.

Encourage me in the silence to find a new home for my heart.

Close the old homes where I knew no solace.

Open me to the future that starts with your voice.

After You Pray

- Sit and listen.

- Write what you hear, sense, see.

- Create something.

- Keep praying.

- Write your own prayer.

LISTENING

Before You Pray

- Choose a time to pray.

- Choose a place to pray.

- Use the words, lines, or complete prayers in the offerings in the book.

- Acknowledge your distractions and that they're real.

- Excuse your distractions and let them know you'll return to them.

- Gently engage the practice in God's presence.

When You Pray

Inside me is your voice not just my own.

Within me is an inner wisdom resembling the sacred.

I want to hear that inner teacher.

That voice will tell me I've done it wrong as many times as it'll tell me that I've done it well.

The problem is not in the voice or in what's said.

The problem is in my hearing.

The problem is with my attendance to what truth has been given.

The truth as it's been given is my gift.

In this silence, help me to hear what's said.

The good, the bad, the truth. Help me to receive what I hear as true.

After You Pray

- Sit and listen.

- Write what you hear, sense, see.

- Create something.

- Keep praying.

- Write your own prayer.

WISDOM OF WORDS

Before You Pray

- Choose a time to pray.

- Choose a place to pray.

- Use the words, lines, or complete prayers in the offerings in the book.

- Acknowledge your distractions and that they're real.

- Excuse your distractions and let them know you'll return to them.

- Gently engage the practice in God's presence.

When You Pray

Thank you for the wisdom of words, for the wonders from them.

You've opened the world to me through what you've said.

You've blessed me with the wealthy words of others.

I hear wells of blessing from so many people and places.

Today I want to hear from you.

I want to attend to the abiding wisdom of your words.

Set them upon my heart.

Make your words heavy the way love can be heavy.

Make me thrive under the heaviness of love and not imprisoned under love's imposters.

Speak to me from the wells of your wisdom.

Make certain that I'm open to receive.

After You Pray

- Sit and listen.

- Write what you hear, sense, see.

- Create something.

- Keep praying.

- Write your own prayer.

UNHELPFUL WORDS

Before You Pray

- Choose a time to pray.

- Choose a place to pray.

- Use the words, lines, or complete prayers in the offerings in the book.

- Acknowledge your distractions and that they're real.

- Excuse your distractions and let them know you'll return to them.

- Gently engage the practice in God's presence.

When You Pray

I've held them in my ears for years.

It feels like I've clasped my hands around my ears.

I've covered them to keep the unhelpful words inside.

I've not been able to open my hands.

I've not been able to free myself of those old words.

They stick around longer, and somehow I hold them closer than the helpful words.

Why am I protective of them?

Why am I helping them stay?

In the quiet, help me to relinquish what I've held so long and so closely.

Your power is great and it is gentle.

In your way, pry from my clenched hands and from my stuck ears the words that I seem to be committed to.

After You Pray

- Sit and listen.

- Write what you hear, sense, see.

- Create something.

- Keep praying.

- Write your own prayer.

WHEN MY SPIRIT CLOSES

Before You Pray

- Choose a time to pray.

- Choose a place to pray.

- Use the words, lines, or complete prayers in the offerings in the book.

- Acknowledge your distractions and that they're real.

- Excuse your distractions and let them know you'll return to them.

- Gently engage the practice in God's presence.

When You Pray

I shrank when I heard the criticism.

My spirit closed because I believed what I heard.

I believed them and not you.

Show me that people are not the only ones worth hearing.

Convince me that you, your voice, and your spirit are worth hearing.

Convince me that when people's estimations differ from yours, I must be brave to side with you.

When my spirit closes because of what well-intentioned people have said;

When my spirit closes because of what mean-hearted people have said;

When my spirit closes because I've let others have my ear, turn me to you.

Open up to you in that strong, repentant way.

I want to turn to you.

I want to open my spirit to you.

After You Pray

- Sit and listen.

- Write what you hear, sense, see.

- Create something.

- Keep praying.

- Write your own prayer.

EARLY GLIMPSES

Before You Pray

- Choose a time to pray.

- Choose a place to pray.

- Use the words, lines, or complete prayers in the offerings in the book.

- Acknowledge your distractions and that they're real.

- Excuse your distractions and let them know you'll return to them.

- Gently engage the practice in God's presence.

When You Pray

I knew early that words had power.

In church and at home and in choral performances, I listened and I was convinced early that speaking well, speaking confidently, and speaking with strength brought good.

I hold those in precious ways.

And I want to reconnect with other early glimpses, the glimpses showing the power of you coming in a different way.

My sense is that I've been too convinced of the power of speech because I'm struggling to believe there's power in silence.

Help me hold these two gestures in a dance.

Help me see power in both.

After You Pray

- Sit and listen.

- Write what you hear, sense, see.

- Create something.

- Keep praying.

- Write your own prayer.

DEEPENING THE QUIET

Before You Pray

- Choose a time to pray.

- Choose a place to pray.

- Use the words, lines, or complete prayers in the offerings in the book.

- Acknowledge your distractions and that they're real.

- Excuse your distractions and let them know you'll return to them.

- Gently engage the practice in God's presence.

When You Pray

Deepen the tones in my soul.

Play the strings within my heart.

Let me hear how my deeps call out to yours.

Free me of the need to speak, of the compulsion to talk, and of the temptation to prove myself.

Invite me into the full musical arrangement that can only come from silence.

Grant me the open ears that will hear in that silence.

Let me sit with the richness of my soul as I reach out to the One from whom all music comes.

In the quiet, let me hear you. In the deepening quiet, sing to me.

After You Pray

- Sit and listen.

- Write what you hear, sense, see.

- Create something.

- Keep praying.

- Write your own prayer.

IN THE DARK

Before You Pray

- Choose a time to pray.

- Choose a place to pray.

- Use the words, lines, or complete prayers in the offerings in the book.

- Acknowledge your distractions and that they're real.

- Excuse your distractions and let them know you'll return to them.

- Gently engage the practice in God's presence.

When You Pray

The problem with trusting you is the darkness.

I can't see you or the thing, the person, the idea in which you're calling me to trust.

I can't know from seeing or touching that
something's really there.

I'm feeling faith and there's often no feeling
to something undiscovered and unreached.

The dark and dismal presence without
presence.

The felt and known but somehow still unseen.

Faith—in a walk or a life or a relationship or
in you—stretches me.

It's making me into someone I haven't been.

In this darkness show me how to be a person
I've never been.

Show me how to have courage for me, the
person who is still forming.

Help me enter into the darkness of quiet.

Help me while I'm there.

After You Pray

- Sit and listen.

- Write what you hear, sense, see.

- Create something.

- Keep praying.

- Write your own prayer.

INDWELLING

Before You Pray

- Choose a time to pray.

- Choose a place to pray.

- Use the words, lines, or complete prayers in the offerings in the book.

- Acknowledge your distractions and that they're real.

- Excuse your distractions and let them know you'll return to them.

- Gently engage the practice in God's presence.

When You Pray

Come to me.

Know me.

Make room in me.

Live in me.

Stretch out in me.

Rest in me.

Be comfortable in me.

Abide in me.

Indwell me.

After You Pray

- Sit and listen.

- Write what you hear, sense, see.

- Create something.

- Keep praying.

- Write your own prayer.

COME

Before You Pray

- Choose a time to pray.

- Choose a place to pray.

- Use the words, lines, or complete prayers in the offerings in the book.

- Acknowledge your distractions and that they're real.

- Excuse your distractions and let them know you'll return to them.

- Gently engage the practice in God's presence.

When You Pray

Come when I expect you.

Come when I can't pray.

Come when all feels good.

Come because nothing works.

Come so I know you're near.

Come when I doubt your existence.

Come at the last moment.

Come at the beginning of every day.

Come when nothing else does.

Come and stay.

After You Pray

- Sit and listen.

- Write what you hear, sense, see.

- Create something.

- Keep praying.

- Write your own prayer.

PRAYERS FOR DISCERNMENT

"In fact, the spiritual journey can be understood as the movement from seeing God nowhere, or seeing God only where we expect to see him, to seeing God everywhere, especially where we least expect him."

Ruth Haley Barton, *Pursuing God's Will Together*, 20

THOSE FEARS ARE REAL

Before You Pray

- Choose a time to pray.

- Choose a place to pray.

- Use the words, lines, or complete prayers in the offerings in the book.

- Acknowledge your distractions and that they're real.

- Excuse your distractions and let them know you'll return to them.

- Gently engage the practice in God's presence.

When You Pray

Those fears are real.

The ones I show and the ones I hide.

I'm aware of many of them, and some of them are smarter than me still.

Whether I see them and know them, they are real.

Make me aware the story of my fears, their origins and their destinies.

My fears are real, as are their origins and their futures.

Convince me of the future you've sketched for me.

The faith there, the wonder there, the playful creativity there.

All of those are real, too.

After You Pray

- Sit and listen.

- Write what you hear, sense, see.

- Create something.

- Keep praying.

- Write your own prayer.

IMAGINING A BEGINNING

Before You Pray

- Choose a time to pray.

- Choose a place to pray.

- Use the words, lines, or complete prayers in the offerings in the book.

- Acknowledge your distractions and that they're real.

- Excuse your distractions and let them know you'll return to them.

- Gently engage the practice in God's presence.

When You Pray

I know what I've released, what I've let go of, what I've left.

I'm well-acquainted with what's behind me.

Like a familiar song I keep hearing, I'm tempted to keep pressing play to all those familiar tunes from my yesterdays.

There's security in things I've ended.

It's the beginnings that are troubling me.

Imagining a beginning when all I hear is from before is what catches me and pulls me down.

Lift me so that I can imagine beyond what I've been.

Free me.

After You Pray

- Sit and listen.

- Write what you hear, sense, see.

- Create something.

- Keep praying.

- Write your own prayer.

RENEWED VISION

Before You Pray

- Choose a time to pray.

- Choose a place to pray.

- Use the words, lines, or complete prayers in the offerings in the book.

- Acknowledge your distractions and that they're real.

- Excuse your distractions and let them know you'll return to them.

- Gently engage the practice in God's presence.

When You Pray

I want to see.

For so long, I've seen dim pictures.

Change my eyes.

Change my sight.

Change my vision.

I want to see what you see.

I want to see as you see.

I want to see.

After You Pray

- Sit and listen.

- Write what you hear, sense, see.

- Create something.

- Keep praying.

- Write your own prayer.

WHAT'S NEXT?

Before You Pray

- Choose a time to pray.

- Choose a place to pray.

- Use the words, lines, or complete prayers in the offerings in the book.

- Acknowledge your distractions and that they're real.

- Excuse your distractions and let them know you'll return to them.

- Gently engage the practice in God's presence.

When You Pray

I don't know what's next.

I know that behind me is a series of interruptions to my plans.

I know that around me a circle of dashed hopes.

I know that inside my soul is loss and gain.

I'm unsure what to expect.

I'm even wondering whether you'll be near in a life of unanswered questions.

It's frustrating not having answers.

Sitting with you is like that.

All those minutes of waiting remind me that I am alone.

And yet I'm not alone.

I'm accompanied in a firm way even if in an invisible way.

In this space of silence, welcome me into your company.

In this quietness, make me know and sense your being present with me.

After You Pray

- Sit and listen.

- Write what you hear, sense, see.

- Create something.

- Keep praying.

- Write your own prayer.

BEING A PERSON OF FAITH

Before You Pray

- Choose a time to pray.

- Choose a place to pray.

- Use the words, lines, or complete prayers in the offerings in the book.

- Acknowledge your distractions and that they're real.

- Excuse your distractions and let them know you'll return to them.

- Gently engage the practice in God's presence.

When You Pray

I like knowing things, having all the answers, and the hardest thing to do is live by the discovery known as faith.

I'm not the believing type, even though I'm a person of faith.

I'm also a person of doubt.

What's as real as my faith is my wondering.

I wonder if you'll act, if you'll speak, if you'll open the way ahead.

I cannot see the grand vista or the humble next steps for that matter.

The future is pulling for me because you've placed things there for me.

I want to believe what's calling me.

I want to believe what I hear is the tone and timber of divinity.

Keep speaking until I find what you've said.

Let the echo of what I hear continue until I find my path.

After You Pray

- Sit and listen.

- Write what you hear, sense, see.

- Create something.

- Keep praying.

- Write your own prayer.

TRUSTING YOU

Before You Pray

- Choose a time to pray.

- Choose a place to pray.

- Use the words, lines, or complete prayers in the offerings in the book.

- Acknowledge your distractions and that they're real.

- Excuse your distractions and let them know you'll return to them.

- Gently engage the practice in God's presence.

When You Pray

I'm feeling the rub between my comfort and my future.

I'm comfortable with what I know, the life that's visible and that's behind me.

I'm comfortable with the life around me.

I know those lives.

But there's more to life than what I've known and where I am.

There's the rub.

Trusting is normal, common, but I'm afraid to trust what you've placed ahead.

My problem is the dark unknown on the bottom of that trust.

The part of me that never really feels comfortable in the unknown world created by trust.

I wonder what you'll do with my doubting you.

I wonder how you'll hold these truths in the quiet between us.

After You Pray

- Sit and listen.

- Write what you hear, sense, see.

- Create something.

- Keep praying.

- Write your own prayer.

ALL GOES QUIET

Before You Pray

- Choose a time to pray.

- Choose a place to pray.

- Use the words, lines, or complete prayers in the offerings in the book.

- Acknowledge your distractions and that they're real.

- Excuse your distractions and let them know you'll return to them.

- Gently engage the practice in God's presence.

When You Pray

When all goes quiet, help me keep listening.

I want to see glimpses of hope.

I want to look around at the faces of my siblings and see connection rather than distance.

We've not truly seen each other.

This day can be different.

Our bonds can tighten and deepen.

The power to see that way and the blessing to view the world like that can only come from you.

The ability to witness love on display is ability that you possess.

Make me capable of seeing.

What I want comes from you.

Who I want to be comes from you.

In this quietness, invite me into those desired outcomes.

In this time of silence, wait with me until I am more deeply who I really am.

After You Pray

- Sit and listen.

- Write what you hear, sense, see.

- Create something.

- Keep praying.

- Write your own prayer.

THIS CHOICE

Before You Pray

- Choose a time to pray.

- Choose a place to pray.

- Use the words, lines, or complete prayers in the offerings in the book.

- Acknowledge your distractions and that they're real.

- Excuse your distractions and let them know you'll return to them.

- Gently engage the practice in God's presence.

When You Pray

This choice is about surrendering what I believe is ahead.

Arrest my anxieties and let me offer them to you.

Turn my worries into prayers.

Transform me so that what's unknown catapults me into praise.

Give me what's in your hand.

I choose trust.

Give me knowledge beyond the answer to my small question.

I choose trust.

Give me what you've provided every other time in my life.

I choose to trust.

After You Pray

- Sit and listen.

- Write what you hear, sense, see.

- Create something.

- Keep praying.

- Write your own prayer.

TEACH US TO PRAY

Before You Pray

- Choose a time to pray.

- Choose a place to pray.

- Use the words, lines, or complete prayers in the offerings in the book.

- Acknowledge your distractions and that they're real.

- Excuse your distractions and let them know you'll return to them.

- Gently engage the practice in God's presence.

When You Pray

The way that son prayed,

The night his father died,

When the doctors kept working,

When their best work failed,

When that son breathed hope,

When I learned his disappointment,

And those nurses switched places

And those doctors traded tasks

And that father heard his son's breaths

And that son waited for you,

When you were there.

Did you answer?

After You Pray

- Sit and listen.

- Write what you hear, sense, see.

- Create something.

- Keep praying.

- Write your own prayer.

OUR COLLECTIVE FUTURE

Before You Pray

- Choose a time to pray.

- Choose a place to pray.

- Use the words, lines, or complete prayers in the offerings in the book.

- Acknowledge your distractions and that they're real.

- Excuse your distractions and let them know you'll return to them.

- Gently engage the practice in God's presence.

When You Pray

Our collective future is in and with and for you.

The truth about me is that I'm included in community.

I'm not alone in my discovery.

I'm accompanied in my discernment.

May you grant me daily a proximity to the tomorrows where you're present.

Give me and us such generous spirits that we pray for the best, seek the good, and persist in the suffering along this way.

Empower the people in my path today to be loving, gracious, good, faithful, and persistent.

They are my reminders of beautiful futures and bright tomorrows.

I am, already and always, in a known and wondrous future because my life ends and doesn't end in you.

After You Pray

- Sit and listen.

- Write what you hear, sense, see.

- Create something.

- Keep praying.

- Write your own prayer.

SURRENDERING ALL

Before You Pray

- Choose a time to pray.

- Choose a place to pray.

- Use the words, lines, or complete prayers in the offerings in the book.

- Acknowledge your distractions and that they're real.

- Excuse your distractions and let them know you'll return to them.

- Gently engage the practice in God's presence.

When You Pray

That song is a judgment and an opportunity.

The one I grew up with about surrendering all.

It feels close and distant during this time of discernment.

It feels best to sing it, best because on some days the words are a dream.

On other days, the words feel like a nightmare.

Surrendering all is my statement of faith. I want to do it.

I desire to surrender.

Surrendering all is my statement of being.

Right now, in this moment, I'm surrendering.

I have no idea about the next moment.

For now, take me as I am. My hands are open.

I'm surrendering what's in them.

After You Pray

- Sit and listen.

- Write what you hear, sense, see.

- Create something.

- Keep praying.

- Write your own prayer.

PRAYERS FOR LOVE

"The word of God penetrates through the thick of human verbosity to the silent center of our heart; silence opens in us the space where the word can be heard…the prayer of the heart in the most profound sense unites mind and heart in the intimacy of the divine love."

Henri Nouwen, *Reaching Out*, 136, 146

BEING IN LOVE

Before You Pray

- Choose a time to pray.

- Choose a place to pray.

- Use the words, lines, or complete prayers in the offerings in the book.

- Acknowledge your distractions and that they're real.

- Excuse your distractions and let them know you'll return to them.

- Gently engage the practice in God's presence.

When You Pray

I began in love, drawing my breath from a Creator who gave his life to me.

I grew by and through love despite every memory to the counter.

I am here because of love's power to keep going and to keep me going.

I am involved in love, surrounded in God who has given his best in Christ to love me.

I am hosted by love so that my days are dressed and decorated with goodness and truth.

I will end in love, finding my eternal future in a perpetual embrace of perfect, fearless love.

After You Pray

- Sit and listen.

- Write what you hear, sense, see.

- Create something.

- Keep praying.

- Write your own prayer.

DEALING WITH HATE

Before You Pray

- Choose a time to pray.

- Choose a place to pray.

- Use the words, lines, or complete prayers in the offerings in the book.

- Acknowledge your distractions and that they're real.

- Excuse your distractions and let them know you'll return to them.

- Gently engage the practice in God's presence.

When You Pray

I am ashamed of it so I must pray about it.

The pain that's turned me to hatred.

Looking at it, I see all the reasons that make hate normal.

I need you to help me look beyond that still picture.

It isn't the best portrait of me.

I am more than my hatred.

I am more than my pain.

I am an instrument of love.

Deal with me.

Deal with my hatred.

So I might live freely.

After You Pray

- Sit and listen.

- Write what you hear, sense, see.

- Create something.

- Keep praying.

- Write your own prayer.

ON THE PATH OF LOVE

Before You Pray

- Choose a time to pray.

- Choose a place to pray.

- Use the words, lines, or complete prayers in the offerings in the book.

- Acknowledge your distractions and that they're real.

- Excuse your distractions and let them know you'll return to them.

- Gently engage the practice in God's presence.

When You Pray

Pebbles under my feet make my gait slower.

They're sharp and oddly shaped.

They hurt.

Help me take my time.

I'm walking toward love.

I'm on the journey of love.

I feel the pebbles and lose the fact that I'm already on the path of love.

After You Pray

- Sit and listen.

- Write what you hear, sense, see.

- Create something.

- Keep praying.

- Write your own prayer.

IDENTITY AS LOVE

Before You Pray

- Choose a time to pray.

- Choose a place to pray.

- Use the words, lines, or complete prayers in the offerings in the book.

- Acknowledge your distractions and that they're real.

- Excuse your distractions and let them know you'll return to them.

- Gently engage the practice in God's presence.

When You Pray

Today I will call myself what you call yourself and my name will be love.

I will know this part of myself even when being love is hard.

You made me in your image so I can look like love.

May your love and your sweet communion, together, be the life-giving force under me.

May I find my help through you, a God of love.

After You Pray

- Sit and listen.

- Write what you hear, sense, see.

- Create something.

- Keep praying.

- Write your own prayer.

SO LOVED THE WORLD

Before You Pray

- Choose a time to pray.

- Choose a place to pray.

- Use the words, lines, or complete prayers in the offerings in the book.

- Acknowledge your distractions and that they're real.

- Excuse your distractions and let them know you'll return to them.

- Gently engage the practice in God's presence.

When You Pray

Use me to save sin-stricken situations from destruction in the world.

Use me to heal sick and diseased relationships between people in the world.

Use me to teach others how to walk the long journey so love extends throughout the world.

Use me to love my friends and enemies so that love permeates communities of the world.

After You Pray

- Sit and listen.

- Write what you hear, sense, see.

- Create something.

- Keep praying.

- Write your own prayer.

PICTURES

Before You Pray

- Choose a time to pray.

- Choose a place to pray.

- Use the words, lines, or complete prayers in the offerings in the book.

- Acknowledge your distractions and that they're real.

- Excuse your distractions and let them know you'll return to them.

- Gently engage the practice in God's presence.

When You Pray

Be my picture of love.

Be my savior who gave all of himself for me, for others, and for the world.

Be my leader who has walked out the path of love before I do.

Be my guide who joins me in the pain and splendor of love.

Be my vision who gives me images to pull me forward.

Be my inspiration when hatred is easy or, worse, when it's convincing.

Be my picture of love.

After You Pray

- Sit and listen.

- Write what you hear, sense, see.

- Create something.

- Keep praying.

- Write your own prayer.

MOMENTS

Before You Pray

- Choose a time to pray.

- Choose a place to pray.

- Use the words, lines, or complete prayers in the offerings in the book.

- Acknowledge your distractions and that they're real.

- Excuse your distractions and let them know you'll return to them.

- Gently engage the practice in God's presence.

When You Pray

When morning light cracks across the sky and I'm alone, meet me.

As the world around me nestles into the last hugs of rest, awaken my spirit.

Awaken me to the generosity that comes when rest hasn't.

Startle my soul with joy as the worries of yesterday try to rise.

Surround me with silence and anticipation.

Coax my fears to their own deep rest.

Still my heart inside warm blankets of grace.

Use courage to guide me.

Prepare me for what's ahead, for every quiet or noisy moment, for every next step.

Find me waiting, in the morning, and ready to love.

After You Pray

- Sit and listen.

- Write what you hear, sense, see.

- Create something.

- Keep praying.

- Write your own prayer.

NOURISHING LOVE

Before You Pray

- Choose a time to pray.

- Choose a place to pray.

- Use the words, lines, or complete prayers in the offerings in the book.

- Acknowledge your distractions and that they're real.

- Excuse your distractions and let them know you'll return to them.

- Gently engage the practice in God's presence.

When You Pray

Words can support love; they can diminish love, too.

Words can crowd my heart as I try to beat through small arguments and large betrayals.

They can pack my view of you with what's familiar and common.

Words stop me in my tracks of pain, confusion, and sorrow.

Sometimes, speaking makes no good sense.

In these next moments, nourish my love in the silence.

Not only can silence reflect the depth of what sustains us but it can also feed us.

This time of silence can equip us so that words, when spoken, carry strength and make strength.

In this quietness, I seek to be open to your unutterable love.

In the silence, I welcome all your nourishing grace.

After You Pray

- Sit and listen.

- Write what you hear, sense, see.

- Create something.

- Keep praying.

- Write your own prayer.

IMITATING LOVE

Before You Pray

- Choose a time to pray.

- Choose a place to pray.

- Use the words, lines, or complete prayers in the offerings in the book.

- Acknowledge your distractions and that they're real.

- Excuse your distractions and let them know you'll return to them.

- Gently engage the practice in God's presence.

When You Pray

Love leaves at the worst times.

I want to love—you, myself, others.

When I want to love and still feel loveless, confusion envelopes me.

Show me how to travel my own loveless roads.

Walk ahead down those roads.

Brighten the dim paths and place ways of love in my reach.

I will look for your example.

I will notice how you've loved.

By your strength, I'll live in love.

After You Pray

- Sit and listen.

- Write what you hear, sense, see.

- Create something.

- Keep praying.

- Write your own prayer.

HEARTBREAK

Before You Pray

- Choose a time to pray.

- Choose a place to pray.

- Use the words, lines, or complete prayers in the offerings in the book.

- Acknowledge your distractions and that they're real.

- Excuse your distractions and let them know you'll return to them.

- Gently engage the practice in God's presence.

When You Pray

Seeing the pieces of what I've given stops all my strength.

I feel plugged and stuffed and empty at my loss.

I am aware of how costly love is.

I'm told you know something about this.

I'm told that you are close to the broken-hearted.

Is it true that your dwelling is with us who've lost spirit?

Surround me and see these pieces sticking up from brown grass.

Envelope me in a circle of something so that brokenness isn't my only companion.

After You Pray

- Sit and listen.

- Write what you hear, sense, see.

- Create something.

- Keep praying.

- Write your own prayer.

MY VISION

Before You Pray

- Choose a time to pray.

- Choose a place to pray.

- Use the words, lines, or complete prayers in the offerings in the book.

- Acknowledge your distractions and that they're real.

- Excuse your distractions and let them know you'll return to them.

- Gently engage the practice in God's presence.

When You Pray

My vision weakens daily.

Strengthen my eyes to see.

My resolve falters because the sin of the world keeps sinning.

Strengthen my eyes to see.

My hunger for good trades with sparks of evil wanting expression.

Strengthen my eyes to see.

My faith in others cracks because others aren't perfect.

Strengthen my eyes to see.

After You Pray

- Sit and listen.

- Write what you hear, sense, see.

- Create something.

- Keep praying.

- Write your own prayer.

PRAYERS FOR WAITING

"But I am suggesting that sensitivity to feelings is essential to this kind of teaching and learning—not only because submerged feelings can undermine learning, but also because feelings are a part of the whole person: we can enter into the relationship called truth only in our wholeness, not with our minds alone. Indeed, our feelings may be more vital to truth than our minds…"

Parker Palmer, *To Know As We Are Known*, 85

HELP ME

Before You Pray

- Choose a time to pray.

- Choose a place to pray.

- Use the words, lines, or complete prayers in the offerings in the book.

- Acknowledge your distractions and that they're real.

- Excuse your distractions and let them know you'll return to them.

- Gently engage the practice in God's presence.

When You Pray

Help me recall the places in my life that I want to

keep close.

Help me to celebrate the beautiful memories behind

me in those places.

I want to carry the good with me today.

I want to be impacted positively by where I've come from.

I want to live today like all those special places make a difference.

You know that there are also pain-filled places behind me.

You know that people have hurt me, left me unnamed or wrongly named.

You know where I've been scarred.

You know me perfectly.

Help me to offer you who I am today, pain and joy, sorrows and hopes.

Help me to live with the good in mind and with the bad surrendered.

Amen.

After You Pray

- Sit and listen.

- Write what you hear, sense, see.

- Create something.

- Keep praying.

- Write your own prayer.

TODAY

Before You Pray

- Choose a time to pray.

- Choose a place to pray.

- Use the words, lines, or complete prayers in the offerings in the book.

- Acknowledge your distractions and that they're real.

- Excuse your distractions and let them know you'll return to them.

- Gently engage the practice in God's presence.

When You Pray

Giver of Good Things,

You know what I desire and what I lack.

My needs are before you, known to you, and important to you.

You have my best desires in your heart.

My dreams are not strange to you.

You call me special no matter what I have.

My lack of this or that doesn't have to keep me distant from you.

Will you lure me into your company today?

Will you keep me close because my poverty makes me feel distant?

Will you be gentle with me when I can't be gentle with myself?

I need your help because I'm susceptible to comparing myself with others.

Make sure I know that I am unique and special to you even in my poverty.

Amen.

After You Pray

- Sit and listen.

- Write what you hear, sense, see.

- Create something.

- Keep praying.

- Write your own prayer.

PERFECT LOVE

Before You Pray

- Choose a time to pray.

- Choose a place to pray.

- Use the words, lines, or complete prayers in the offerings in the book.

- Acknowledge your distractions and that they're real.

- Excuse your distractions and let them know you'll return to them.

- Gently engage the practice in God's presence.

When You Pray

I love well sometimes and at times, I love poorly.

I know of people who would describe me as

unloving.

I think of myself as uncaring sometimes, too.

You love wonderfully.

You accomplish the miracle without effort.

Or maybe it does take work for you to love.

Either way, I want to love better, harder.

Turn me into a fearless lover.

Turn me into the lover that I can be.

Amen.

After You Pray

- Sit and listen.

- Write what you hear, sense, see.

- Create something.

- Keep praying.

- Write your own prayer.

WAITING FOR HEALING

Before You Pray

- Choose a time to pray.

- Choose a place to pray.

- Use the words, lines, or complete prayers in the offerings in the book.

- Acknowledge your distractions and that they're real.

- Excuse your distractions and let them know you'll return to them.

- Gently engage the practice in God's presence.

When You Pray

Notice the years.

Point out what I've forgotten but still somehow

remembered.

Guide me as I consider the pain.

Illuminate the dark and scary paths.

Make sure I know I'm not alone.

Give me someone who can share this burden.

Ready them for the story I have to offer.

Make me aware of you as I talk with them.

Hold my pain through their arms.

Bless me through their hands.

Bless me while I wait.

Amen.

After You Pray

- Sit and listen.

- Write what you hear, sense, see.

- Create something.

- Keep praying.

- Write your own prayer.

PRAYING INTO ME

Before You Pray

- Choose a time to pray.

- Choose a place to pray.

- Use the words, lines, or complete prayers in the offerings in the book.

- Acknowledge your distractions and that they're real.

- Excuse your distractions and let them know you'll return to them.

- Gently engage the practice in God's presence.

When You Pray

I am loved whether or not I pray.

I am wanted even when I mess up and make

mistakes.

I am held close to you despite people trying to say otherwise.

I am yours even if I feel distant.

I am not alone, though almost everything testifies that I am.

I am with you even when I've done my best to run from you.

I am acceptable.

I am loved.

Amen.

After You Pray

- Sit and listen.

- Write what you hear, sense, see.

- Create something.

- Keep praying.

- Write your own prayer.

TEARS

Before You Pray

- Choose a time to pray.

- Choose a place to pray.

- Use the words, lines, or complete prayers in the offerings in the book.

- Acknowledge your distractions and that they're real.

- Excuse your distractions and let them know you'll return to them.

- Gently engage the practice in God's presence.

When You Pray

Scripture says you count my tears.

How many have I shed?

What have I cried about?

Do you remember the pains the way I do?

Have I cried alone or do you cry with me?

Where will I get help for this?

Do you recall the dark nights I've never mentioned?

How does your heart sit with my depths?

Do you care?

What do your tears say about you?

Do you realize how long I've wanted freedom and joy?

When will you heal me, grant me the splendor of a different answer?

After You Pray

- Sit and listen.

- Write what you hear, sense, see.

- Create something.

- Keep praying.

- Write your own prayer.

UNCONDITIONAL

Before You Pray

- Choose a time to pray.

- Choose a place to pray.

- Use the words, lines, or complete prayers in the offerings in the book.

- Acknowledge your distractions and that they're real.

- Excuse your distractions and let them know you'll return to them.

- Gently engage the practice in God's presence.

When You Pray

When I pray, it's hard to be real.

It's hard to get over the voice in my head.

There are things I want to say to you.

Can you silence the internal judgment that comes

when I'm honest?

My faith says you're smart enough to know them.

My faith also says that there's worth in my telling you.

I want you to know these things about me.

I'm afraid to say them for fear that you'll think

differently.

I'm afraid that you may not love me the way

unconditional means you do.

I'm afraid.

Make me courageous.

Make me believe.

After You Pray

- Sit and listen.

- Write what you hear, sense, see.

- Create something.

- Keep praying.

- Write your own prayer.

WHAT I NEED TO TRUST

Before You Pray

- Choose a time to pray.

- Choose a place to pray.

- Use the words, lines, or complete prayers in the offerings in the book.

- Acknowledge your distractions and that they're real.

- Excuse your distractions and let them know you'll return to them.

- Gently engage the practice in God's presence.

When You Pray

Listening Spirit,

You've heard me when others have assumed what I'd say.

You've embraced me, pain and sorrow, breaks and injuries.

In your listening, you've healed me.

In your watching, you've graced me.

In your withholding answers, you've stretched me.

Deepen us.

Help me aim my life toward you, not just your blessings.

Grant that I might hear others the way you hear me.

Give me what I need to trust that you hear and answer all my prayers.

May I wait well.

After You Pray

- Sit and listen.

- Write what you hear, sense, see.

- Create something.

- Keep praying.

- Write your own prayer.

GIVE

Before You Pray

- Choose a time to pray.

- Choose a place to pray.

- Use the words, lines, or complete prayers in the offerings in the book.

- Acknowledge your distractions and that they're real.

- Excuse your distractions and let them know you'll return to them.

- Gently engage the practice in God's presence.

When You Pray

I cannot control what another person thinks of me.

Give me the grace to believe that.

Give me the courage to live without regard for the

thoughts of others.

Give me the sensitivity to care for people nonetheless.

Give me the self-assurance to confide in myself and
to underline my own strengths.

Give me the humility to see how you've made me and
be glad with what I see.

Give me the power to live purposefully, clearly, and
soberly even while I wait for you.

Give me the patience to keep praying through my
anguish and sorrow.

Give me the boldness to believe you love me even
when I don't get what I want.

Give me the strength to speak lovingly to others while
communicating the truth.

After You Pray

- Sit and listen.

- Write what you hear, sense, see.

- Create something.

- Keep praying.

- Write your own prayer.

GOOD NEWS

Before You Pray

- Choose a time to pray.

- Choose a place to pray.

- Use the words, lines, or complete prayers in the offerings in the book.

- Acknowledge your distractions and that they're real.

- Excuse your distractions and let them know you'll return to them.

- Gently engage the practice in God's presence.

When You Pray

I don't need to rehearse the bad words that were

spoken in my ears.

I need to hear the good ones.

I need to hear the good news that you have spoken.

I realize that everything you say won't feel good or

make me feel good.

But everything you say *is good*.

Everything you say about me is good and worth

hearing.

Your words are always constructive.

Help me remember that when I hear the opposite

inside and outside myself.

Everything you say is good news.

After You Pray

- Sit and listen.

- Write what you hear, sense, see.

- Create something.

- Keep praying.

- Write your own prayer.

GROW MY SOUL

Before You Pray

- Choose a time to pray.

- Choose a place to pray.

- Use the words, lines, or complete prayers in the offerings in the book.

- Acknowledge your distractions and that they're real.

- Excuse your distractions and let them know you'll return to them.

- Gently engage the practice in God's presence.

When You Pray

I've been taught things about you that are true and

things that are small.

Enlarge my view of you and grant me increasing

humility to respond in wonder.

Turn to my requests and answer them.

I've been praying for some of the same things for a
long time.

Answer me in whatever creative way you choose.

I want to tell others that you answer.

I want to believe that you're able.

Answer and strengthen my faith in the process.

Grow my soul in the midst of my waiting.

Grow my soul in the midst of the quiet.

After You Pray

- Sit and listen.

- Write what you hear, sense, see.

- Create something.

- Keep praying.

- Write your own prayer.

PRAYERS FOR WORSHIP

"Love is always to be recognized and adored, for it is the signature of God lying upon creation; often smudged and faded, almost blotted out, yet legible to the eyes which have been cleansed by prayer."

Evelyn Underhill, *Abba*, 19

YOU

Before You Pray

- Choose a time to pray.

- Choose a place to pray.

- Use the words, lines, or complete prayers in the offerings in the book.

- Acknowledge your distractions and that they're real.

- Excuse your distractions and let them know you'll return to them.

- Gently engage the practice in God's presence.

When You Pray

You are more than I've ever imagined.

Help me to think better of you.

Help me to find my thoughts poor when I try to collapse you into what I know.

You are beyond what I understand, what I wrap my head around.

Help me lean into the ways you've expressed yourself.

Help me to do so humbly.

You are what you've been.

You are more.

You are always more.

After You Pray

- Sit and listen.

- Write what you hear, sense, see.

- Create something.

- Keep praying.

- Write your own prayer.

WORTH

Before You Pray

- Choose a time to pray.

- Choose a place to pray.

- Use the words, lines, or complete prayers in the offerings in the book.

- Acknowledge your distractions and that they're real.

- Excuse your distractions and let them know you'll return to them.

- Gently engage the practice in God's presence.

When You Pray

You are worth my best praise, my faithful worship.

Expand my word choice so my words increasingly fit.

Focus my attention so I can ascribe worth that's already yours.

Be worthy to me and lovely to me and beyond words
to me.

Show me that my worth comes from you.

Teach me that my value comes from you.

I will settle the questions of my soul because I'm of
value to you.

I will start settling those questions by worshiping you.

After You Pray

- Sit and listen.

- Write what you hear, sense, see.

- Create something.

- Keep praying.

- Write your own prayer.

WHEN I'M CONVINCED

Before You Pray

- Choose a time to pray.

- Choose a place to pray.

- Use the words, lines, or complete prayers in the offerings in the book.

- Acknowledge your distractions and that they're real.

- Excuse your distractions and let them know you'll return to them.

- Gently engage the practice in God's presence.

When You Pray

When I'm convinced I know you, show me more of your character.

When I'm sure that I've figured you out, challenge me with your latest acts in the world.

When I've closed myself off to your wonder, upset me with truth.

When I've settled on my faith, loosen me by your humility.

When I've turned my vision to a small place, envelop me by others who live in you.

When I sit in self-assurance, point out your regular way of coordinating worlds.

When I've stopped learning, pull me into the classrooms of divinity.

After You Pray

- Sit and listen.

- Write what you hear, sense, see.

- Create something.

- Keep praying.

- Write your own prayer.

WHO YOU ARE

Before You Pray

- Choose a time to pray.

- Choose a place to pray.

- Use the words, lines, or complete prayers in the offerings in the book.

- Acknowledge your distractions and that they're real.

- Excuse your distractions and let them know you'll return to them.

- Gently engage the practice in God's presence.

When You Pray

You're my peace when all clamors for my soul

You're my great savior, pulling me from my sins.

You're my faithful friend, showing me fidelity in every gesture.

You're my constant direction, placing me on a sure path.

You're my orientation, my destiny, keeping me focused on real life.

You're the love that endures.

You're the grace that keeps coming.

You're the miracle that brings life.

You're the one I see when I look for help.

You're the one offering help before I ask.

Thank you.

After You Pray

- Sit and listen.

- Write what you hear, sense, see.

- Create something.

- Keep praying.

- Write your own prayer.

VIEW MORE

Before You Pray

- Choose a time to pray.

- Choose a place to pray.

- Use the words, lines, or complete prayers in the offerings in the book.

- Acknowledge your distractions and that they're real.

- Excuse your distractions and let them know you'll return to them.

- Gently engage the practice in God's presence.

When You Pray

Those two words become my ready prayer.

I'm finding myself feeling them, thinking them, contemplating them.

View more.

With them I hold a basic request that continues to flourish in my depths.

I want to view more, to see more, and to gain a vision that, until now, I've missed.

Grant me and those I love generous eyes, eyes that can take in what's real and true and present.

I embrace what's in your hand: larger views.

In my time of centering today, I will keep looking, keep listening, and keep viewing more.

After You Pray

- Sit and listen.

- Write what you hear, sense, see.

- Create something.

- Keep praying.

- Write your own prayer.

IF YOU STOPPED

Before You Pray

- Choose a time to pray.

- Choose a place to pray.

- Use the words, lines, or complete prayers in the offerings in the book.

- Acknowledge your distractions and that they're real.

- Excuse your distractions and let them know you'll return to them.

- Gently engage the practice in God's presence.

When You Pray

If you stopped, we'd live on the echo of songs you've sang about creation.

If you stopped, we'd pull from every last memory and speak of your goodness.

If you stopped, we'd sit in the quiet of grief and the noise of perpetual praise.

If you stopped, we'd look for another and come up short.

If you stopped, we'd wait in faith believing that all you've done has to continue.

After You Pray

- Sit and listen.

- Write what you hear, sense, see.

- Create something.

- Keep praying.

- Write your own prayer.

JOHN 11 BREATH PRAYERS

Before You Pray

- Choose a time to pray.

- Choose a place to pray.

- Use the words, lines, or complete prayers in the offerings in the book.

- Acknowledge your distractions and that they're real.

- Excuse your distractions and let them know you'll return to them.

- Gently engage the practice in God's presence.

When You Pray

I'm hearing what you told me.

I believe in you through this.

Help me see the glory.

Help me spot the splendor.

I ask for grace to notice your Presence.

After You Pray

- Sit and listen.

- Write what you hear, sense, see.

- Create something.

- Keep praying.

- Write your own prayer.

SELECT IMAGES OF GOD

Before You Pray

- Choose a time to pray.

- Choose a place to pray.

- Use the words, lines, or complete prayers in the offerings in the book.

- Acknowledge your distractions and that they're real.

- Excuse your distractions and let them know you'll return to them.

- Gently engage the practice in God's presence.

When You Pray

Rock

Help

Healer

Strength

Rescue

Faithful Friend

Mighty God

Wonderful Counselor

Inner Witness

Prince of Peace

Ancient of Days

Spirit of Grace

Bread of Life

All I Need

Holy One of Israel

Mother to the Motherless

Father to the Fatherless

Wisdom of the Ages

After You Pray

- Sit and listen.

- Write what you hear, sense, see.

- Create something.

- Keep praying.

- Write your own prayer.

THREATEN ALL I WORSHIP

Before You Pray

- Choose a time to pray.

- Choose a place to pray.

- Use the words, lines, or complete prayers in the offerings in the book.

- Acknowledge your distractions and that they're real.

- Excuse your distractions and let them know you'll return to them.

- Gently engage the practice in God's presence.

When You Pray

You are a threat to all I worship.

My grip is tight around my gods.

I've put many deities before you.

The more I pray, the clearer my sin.

Forgive me by snatching those gods.

Wash me by showing their impotence.

Cleanse me by breaking them.

Perfect me by showing me who is true.

Stabilize me in your presence.

Show me what God looks like.

After You Pray

- Sit and listen.

- Write what you hear, sense, see.

- Create something.

- Keep praying.

- Write your own prayer.

GREATNESS

Before You Pray

- Choose a time to pray.

- Choose a place to pray.

- Use the words, lines, or complete prayers in the offerings in the book.

- Acknowledge your distractions and that they're real.

- Excuse your distractions and let them know you'll return to them.

- Gently engage the practice in God's presence.

When You Pray

Take my small views of Jesus.

Today place your hands on them.

Disassemble each one.

Show me the pieces.

Lift up their inherent poverty.

Crush them.

Bury my idols.

In doing so, bless me.

Open me to who you are.

Offer me views of your greatness.

Teach me who you are.

Convince of your wideness and depth.

So that I may worship you.

After You Pray

- Sit and listen.

- Write what you hear, sense, see.

- Create something.

- Keep praying.

- Write your own prayer.

FIRST

Before You Pray

- Choose a time to pray.

- Choose a place to pray.

- Use the words, lines, or complete prayers in the offerings in the book.

- Acknowledge your distractions and that they're real.

- Excuse your distractions and let them know you'll return to them.

- Gently engage the practice in God's presence.

When You Pray

You are important to me

You are necessary to me

You are life-giving to me

I put people in your place

I put tasks in your place

I put desires in your place

You are important

You are necessary

You are life-giving

More than good work which might help
others

More than noble acts which might expand
kindness

You are

You are

You are

If I stay, work, succeed, or fail

You

You

You

After You Pray

- Sit and listen.

- Write what you hear, sense, see.

- Create something.

- Keep praying.

- Write your own prayer.

PRAYERS FOR PEACE

"...God does not and will not abandon us. God's commitment, that is, God's love for us, is steadfast. And so it is that God is committed to us in our very world, even unto the cross."

Kelly Brown Douglas, "Meditation on Good Friday," National Cathedral Church, April 14, 2017

BE PEACE

Before You Pray

- Choose a time to pray.

- Choose a place to pray.

- Use the words, lines, or complete prayers in the offerings in the book.

- Acknowledge your distractions and that they're real.

- Excuse your distractions and let them know you'll return to them.

- Gently engage the practice in God's presence.

When You Pray

The cluster of feelings makes trouble my soul's closest companion.

You see the list.

It's long, all those feelings.

It's hard, all that truth.

And it's the truth between us.

I need a prince, a companion, a friend.

I need peace.

Be those needed things.

Bring peace.

Be peace.

After You Pray

- Sit and listen.

- Write what you hear, sense, see.

- Create something.

- Keep praying.

- Write your own prayer.

WITHIN MY SOUL

Before You Pray

- Choose a time to pray.

- Choose a place to pray.

- Use the words, lines, or complete prayers in the offerings in the book.

- Acknowledge your distractions and that they're real.

- Excuse your distractions and let them know you'll return to them.

- Gently engage the practice in God's presence.

When You Pray

The waters of my soul are troubled.

Bring calm to me.

Let me hold it.

Let me breathe it in.

The rage of all those feelings worry me.

Bring peace to me.

Let me accept it.

Let me trade it for the fright.

The waves of fear surround me.

Bring strength to me.

Let me feel it.

Let me dress myself, my soul in its armor.

After You Pray

- Sit and listen.

- Write what you hear, sense, see.

- Create something.

- Keep praying.

- Write your own prayer.

NEW IMAGES

Before You Pray

- Choose a time to pray.

- Choose a place to pray.

- Use the words, lines, or complete prayers in the offerings in the book.

- Acknowledge your distractions and that they're real.

- Excuse your distractions and let them know you'll return to them.

- Gently engage the practice in God's presence.

When You Pray

I'm open to your images of peace.

I'm committing to new images of restoration.

I am in your hands, knowing that you bring rest with your embrace.

Replace what I've been loyal to, the varied embraces that no longer work.

Trade my views of life in your will with new pictures, pictures of loyalty to love.

You came to bring life, abundant and full life.

I've often downgraded what you've brought.

But I'm dissatisfied with impersonating life.

I'm ready for an upgrade that returns me to your splendid abundance.

I'm committed to embracing that abundance and to living in peace.

I'm committed to living at peace where peace is my new address.

After You Pray

- Sit and listen.

- Write what you hear, sense, see.

- Create something.

- Keep praying.

- Write your own prayer.

KEEP MY SOUL

Before You Pray

- Choose a time to pray.

- Choose a place to pray.

- Use the words, lines, or complete prayers in the offerings in the book.

- Acknowledge your distractions and that they're real.

- Excuse your distractions and let them know you'll return to them.

- Gently engage the practice in God's presence.

When You Pray

Keep my soul

    from dangers seen and unseen.

Keep my spirit

    from the torments that diminish me.

Keep my life

    until I'm only alive and full of life.

Keep my vision

    so I have increasing insight into what's ahead.

Keep my hand

    and make me an instrument of reclamation in your world.

After You Pray

- Sit and listen.

- Write what you hear, sense, see.

- Create something.

- Keep praying.

- Write your own prayer.

TIMES OF VIOLENCE

Before You Pray

- Choose a time to pray.

- Choose a place to pray.

- Use the words, lines, or complete prayers in the offerings in the book.

- Acknowledge your distractions and that they're real.

- Excuse your distractions and let them know you'll return to them.

- Gently engage the practice in God's presence.

When You Pray

I don't know that I believe you're in this.

I don't know that I believe that peace matters to you.

When the bodies of my community's children are displayed like trophies of blood and not of gold or silver;

When our bodies are hoisted on gurneys and ambulances only to be shelved in morgues and buried in cemeteries;

When the news reports body counts the way it does the weather;

I am not sure you are for peace.

Search me and find where I've been too hurt to trust you.

Heal me.

Heal us.

Make me an agent of healing.

After You Pray

- Sit and listen.

- Write what you hear, sense, see.

- Create something.

- Keep praying.

- Write your own prayer.

TRAUMAS

Before You Pray

- Choose a time to pray.

- Choose a place to pray.

- Use the words, lines, or complete prayers in the offerings in the book.

- Acknowledge your distractions and that they're real.

- Excuse your distractions and let them know you'll return to them.

- Gently engage the practice in God's presence.

When You Pray

Her face leaves only because I still hear her voice.

Her scream returns sometimes, deep and piercing.

Do you hear her the way I still do?

After You Pray

- Sit and listen.

- Write what you hear, sense, see.

- Create something.

- Keep praying.

- Write your own prayer.

WHEN I SIT

Before You Pray

- Choose a time to pray.

- Choose a place to pray.

- Use the words, lines, or complete prayers in the offerings in the book.

- Acknowledge your distractions and that they're real.

- Excuse your distractions and let them know you'll return to them.

- Gently engage the practice in God's presence.

When You Pray

When I sit, relieve me of my need to accomplish.

Trim me of the needs to do, achieve, and create in order to prove my existence.

Remove as much as possible my need to please—even to please you.

Grant me a need to be *at* peace.

Help me to sit in peace.

When I sit, let me fall into a peace that passes all understanding.

After You Pray

- Sit and listen.

- Write what you hear, sense, see.

- Create something.

- Keep praying.

- Write your own prayer.

BREATHING

Before You Pray

- Choose a time to pray.

- Choose a place to pray.

- Use the words, lines, or complete prayers in the offerings in the book.

- Acknowledge your distractions and that they're real.

- Excuse your distractions and let them know you'll return to them.

- Gently engage the practice in God's presence.

When You Pray

Peace that passes all I know

    Brings me help when I need it most

Peace that passes all I know

    Replenishes my soul, preserves my life

Peace that passes all I know

Grants me strength when I'm weak

Peace that passes all I know

Relieves my heart of all strife

Peace that passes all I know

Opens me to the Spirit I seek

Peace that passes all I know

Centers me, sits me near my gracious Host

After You Pray

- Sit and listen.

- Write what you hear, sense, see.

- Create something.

- Keep praying.

- Write your own prayer.

MIDDLES

Before You Pray

- Choose a time to pray.

- Choose a place to pray.

- Use the words, lines, or complete prayers in the offerings in the book.

- Acknowledge your distractions and that they're real.

- Excuse your distractions and let them know you'll return to them.

- Gently engage the practice in God's presence.

When You Pray

All those dark spots that make me wonder if I'll ever rest

All those liminal spaces that took my identity, left me changed

All those middles where I no longer stood close to *before* and couldn't reach *after*

All those places I needed an anchor in the midst of movement

All those times when we sang muffled hymns of blues and lament

All those moments when our plate for filled with sour fruit

All those middles where we couldn't sense good or justice or hope

All those environments which rehearsed pain

Center yourself, O God, in those spaces

Center yourself, O God, in those places

Center yourself, O God, in those spots

Center yourself, O God, in those times

Center yourself, O God, in those moments

Center yourself, O God, in those middles

Center yourself, O God, in those environments

When I travel and fall in the midst of hard life, be in those middles.

After You Pray

- Sit and listen.

- Write what you hear, sense, see.

- Create something.

- Keep praying.

- Write your own prayer.

CIRCLES OF GOD'S COMPANY

Before You Pray

- Choose a time to pray.

- Choose a place to pray.

- Use the words, lines, or complete prayers in the offerings in the book.

- Acknowledge your distractions and that they're real.

- Excuse your distractions and let them know you'll return to them.

- Gently engage the practice in God's presence.

When You Pray

I am surrounded, encircled, enveloped.

When I turn my eyes, I see you dancing.

When I close my eyes, I imagine the blessed movement quickening.

We are surrounded in God's company.

We are encircled in divine community.

We are inside the life of God.

Worlds around us shake.

You continue to dance.

Communities erupt from and in pain.

You envelope each of us in your twirling.

Families break under pressure and grief.

You encircle everyone in the company that distributes wonder.

After You Pray

- Sit and listen.

- Write what you hear, sense, see.

- Create something.

- Keep praying.

- Write your own prayer.

PRAYERS FOR SUFFERING

"In the final analysis, to believe in God means to live our life as a gift from God and to look upon everything that happens in it as a manifestation of this gift...my intention is to penetrate to the deepest meaning of history, and, in the words of Ignatius of Loyola, to "find God in all things."

Gustavo Gutierrez, *We Drink from Our Own Wells*, 110

CHANGING

Before You Pray

- Choose a time to pray.

- Choose a place to pray.

- Use the words, lines, or complete prayers in the offerings in the book.

- Acknowledge your distractions and that they're real.

- Excuse your distractions and let them know you'll return to them.

- Gently engage the practice in God's presence.

When You Pray

This experience is changing me.

I may not be the same.

I've spent a lot of life trying not to change.

If I'm changed, change with me.

Or, if I'm changed, stay unchanged.

Or, if I'm changed and have no clue what I need, be smarter than me.

This experience is changing me.

At least keep this truth true: God is with me.

After You Pray

- Sit and listen.

- Write what you hear, sense, see.

- Create something.

- Keep praying.

- Write your own prayer.

THE PRESENCE

Before You Pray

- Choose a time to pray.

- Choose a place to pray.

- Use the words, lines, or complete prayers in the offerings in the book.

- Acknowledge your distractions and that they're real.

- Excuse your distractions and let them know you'll return to them.

- Gently engage the practice in God's presence.

When You Pray

Sometimes I call you the presence.

It captures that list of names from the bible, from my life.

It says where you are.

It says what you do.

It says how you persist during hard life.

Surround me in your presence.

Surround me in your hospitality.

Surround me in your grace.

Surround me.

After You Pray

- Sit and listen.

- Write what you hear, sense, see.

- Create something.

- Keep praying.

- Write your own prayer.

ANGUISH

Before You Pray

- Choose a time to pray.

- Choose a place to pray.

- Use the words, lines, or complete prayers in the offerings in the book.

- Acknowledge your distractions and that they're real.

- Excuse your distractions and let them know you'll return to them.

- Gently engage the practice in God's presence.

When You Pray

Ready me in this anguish.

Don't let it be worthless.

Create something from it.

Make yourself known through it.

Deepen me and my me-ness.

Settle the parts of my soul that waver.

Somehow use it.

Convert it to energy like Mr. Martin talked about in science class at Simeon.

Transform it the way Mr. Tracy said energy changed when teaching Physics I couldn't grasp.

This pain stills my soul.

It makes me think you're gone.

It makes me believe you've left.

But you're there, in it.

You're readying me.

After You Pray

- Sit and listen.

- Write what you hear, sense, see.

- Create something.

- Keep praying.

- Write your own prayer.

THIS PRESENT TIME

Before You Pray

- Choose a time to pray.

- Choose a place to pray.

- Use the words, lines, or complete prayers in the offerings in the book.

- Acknowledge your distractions and that they're real.

- Excuse your distractions and let them know you'll return to them.

- Gently engage the practice in God's presence.

When You Pray

The sufferings of this present time weigh me down.

Free me from them.

Liberate us from these burdens.

Break our community from what binds us.

Pull from our shoulders the garments of prison, the clothes of restriction.

Snap the chains of indifference that make us settled and comfortable.

The sufferings of this present time are not worthy of us.

They aren't worthy of you.

They aren't worth comparing with your divine intention.

Take us through this present time.

Walk us into tomorrow.

Accompany us into splendor.

After You Pray

- Sit and listen.

- Write what you hear, sense, see.

- Create something.

- Keep praying.

- Write your own prayer.

JESUS

Before You Pray

- Choose a time to pray.

- Choose a place to pray.

- Use the words, lines, or complete prayers in the offerings in the book.

- Acknowledge your distractions and that they're real.

- Excuse your distractions and let them know you'll return to them.

- Gently engage the practice in God's presence.

When You Pray

Jesus, make me a worshipper whose sufferings bccomc part of a redeemed life.

After You Pray

- Sit and listen.

- Write what you hear, sense, see.

- Create something.

- Keep praying.

- Write your own prayer.

SHAME

Before You Pray

- Choose a time to pray.

- Choose a place to pray.

- Use the words, lines, or complete prayers in the offerings in the book.

- Acknowledge your distractions and that they're real.

- Excuse your distractions and let them know you'll return to them.

- Gently engage the practice in God's presence.

When You Pray

I am not what I did.

I am what you did.

I am the image of God.

I am the expression of divinity.

I am the power of grace.

I am love on display.

I am more than I think.

I am a blessing.

I am good.

After You Pray

- Sit and listen.

- Write what you hear, sense, see.

- Create something.

- Keep praying.

- Write your own prayer.

SICKNESS

Before You Pray

- Choose a time to pray.

- Choose a place to pray.

- Use the words, lines, or complete prayers in the offerings in the book.

- Acknowledge your distractions and that they're real.

- Excuse your distractions and let them know you'll return to them.

- Gently engage the practice in God's presence.

When You Pray

Give your closest ear as I whisper my questions, my dreams, and my pains.

Notice the course before me.

Collect my words, gestures, and aches.

Translate them into beautiful, powerful speech.

Be moved by them to act.

Be moved me to swiftly and bless me.

Let me sense your company through what feels like both a crowded and lonely time.

Be in glances and whispers and surprises and meals and silence.

There is room for you as I heal to visit me in so many places.

After You Pray

- Sit and listen.

- Write what you hear, sense, see.

- Create something.

- Keep praying.

- Write your own prayer.

PATIENT CARE

Before You Pray

- Choose a time to pray.

- Choose a place to pray.

- Use the words, lines, or complete prayers in the offerings in the book.

- Acknowledge your distractions and that they're real.

- Excuse your distractions and let them know you'll return to them.

- Gently engage the practice in God's presence.

When You Pray

As I walk into the room, remind me

    I am accompanied

    I am greeted

    I am hosted

I am loved

I am accepted

I am received

I am enriched

I am used

I am blessed

I am sent

Into the next place with more.

After You Pray

- Sit and listen.

- Write what you hear, sense, see.

- Create something.

- Keep praying.

- Write your own prayer.

CROSSING, COMMITTING, AND CARRYING

Before You Pray

- Choose a time to pray.

- Choose a place to pray.

- Use the words, lines, or complete prayers in the offerings in the book.

- Acknowledge your distractions and that they're real.

- Excuse your distractions and let them know you'll return to them.

- Gently engage the practice in God's presence.

When You Pray

Every time I sit in the silence, I'm taking my cross.

Every time I sit in the silence, I'm committing to you, Jesus.

Every time I sit in the silence, I'm holding what I'll carry.

I'm taking my cross.

I'm committing to be with you, Jesus.

I'm carrying what you carried.

I'm accompanying you in this.

You're accompanying me in this.

After You Pray

- Sit and listen.

- Write what you hear, sense, see.

- Create something.

- Keep praying.

- Write your own prayer.

UNSEEN FUTURES

Before You Pray

- Choose a time to pray.

- Choose a place to pray.

- Use the words, lines, or complete prayers in the offerings in the book.

- Acknowledge your distractions and that they're real.

- Excuse your distractions and let them know you'll return to them.

- Gently engage the practice in God's presence.

When You Pray

The dark cloak of pain hides what's next.

There may be more pain.

Trouble may await.

Death may come.

I cannot see.

I don't know the future.

I know you.

You know me.

The future is seen.

The future is safe.

We are there, in the future, together.

After You Pray

- Sit and listen.

- Write what you hear, sense, see.

- Create something.

- Keep praying.

- Write your own prayer.

SLOW REPENTANCE OF SLOW SIN

Before You Pray

- Choose a time to pray.

- Choose a place to pray.

- Use the words, lines, or complete prayers in the offerings in the book.

- Acknowledge your distractions and that they're real.

- Excuse your distractions and let them know you'll return to them.

- Gently engage the practice in God's presence.

When You Pray

God of life,

You know my life,

The events that make my days.

Re-make me daily.

Let the life I have be real life.

Train my concerns with eternity.

Free me from the stress of worrying.

Unshackle my heart.

Open me to the unrestrained grace

You keep offering all the time.

Forgive me of my sins.

Take me over my failures slowly.

Triumph in me and through me.

Where I break the spirit of others,

When I overlook people I should love,

If I let my family down,

Tell me every truth about myself

Grow me up into living Spirit-led life.

The kind that has one source,

Which like a fresh-flowing river

Unsettles, replenishes, wets, moves, and changes.

After You Pray

- Sit and listen.

- Write what you hear, sense, see.

- Create something.

- Keep praying.

- Write your own prayer.

PRAYERS FOR CREATIVITY

Perhaps God is not silent but rather is waiting—
waiting for human beings to gather their thoughts,
compose themselves, regain their speech, and find
their way back into the give-and-take of intimacy with
God.

Renita Weems, *Listening for God*, 67

THE CHAOS

Before You Pray

- Choose a time to pray.

- Choose a place to pray.

- Use the words, lines, or complete prayers in the offerings in the book.

- Acknowledge your distractions and that they're real.

- Excuse your distractions and let them know you'll return to them.

- Gently engage the practice in God's presence.

When You Pray

The scriptures say you hovered over the chaos.

Just prior to creation, however long prior was, you were in it.

You were acquainted with everything that came with nothing.

When there was only you and what you imagined, you were present.

Hover over the world within me, the world of uncertainty, of waiting, of possibility.

Keep me in this current moment, unsettling as it is.

Ground me.

Place my feet on the bottom of nothingness.

Teach me to see.

Teach me to wait in the chaos.

Place me where you've been at such times of possibility.

After You Pray

- Sit and listen.

- Write what you hear, sense, see.

- Create something.

- Keep praying.

- Write your own prayer.

WAITING FOR YOU

Before You Pray

- Choose a time to pray.

- Choose a place to pray.

- Use the words, lines, or complete prayers in the offerings in the book.

- Acknowledge your distractions and that they're real.

- Excuse your distractions and let them know you'll return to them.

- Gently engage the practice in God's presence.

When You Pray

I'm waiting for you.

My hands are ready.

My heart is full.

My spirit is open.

My soul is still.

I'm releasing my hopes into your hands.

I give you my love to take as your own.

I'm waiting to create the way you do.

After You Pray

- Sit and listen.

- Write what you hear, sense, see.

- Create something.

- Keep praying.

- Write your own prayer.

WHEN

Before You Pray

- Choose a time to pray.

- Choose a place to pray.

- Use the words, lines, or complete prayers in the offerings in the book.

- Acknowledge your distractions and that they're real.

- Excuse your distractions and let them know you'll return to them.

- Gently engage the practice in God's presence.

When You Pray

When anticipations which once gave hope have fallen away;

When the dreams which decorated my imaginations have turned;

When the efforts and energies which once swelled purpose in me have drowned in reality;

When rejection has convinced me that the full space of received creativity is too crowded and the consistent whispers of friends is forgotten;

When passion has been misplaced, misdirected, and misshaped;

Grant me the ever-increasing melody that will not go unheard, the rumble of an instrument underneath my feet, the blaring of an unseen horn, the striking of unseen strings.

After You Pray

- Sit and listen.

- Write what you hear, sense, see.

- Create something.

- Keep praying.

- Write your own prayer.

MAKING MUSIC

Before You Pray

- Choose a time to pray.

- Choose a place to pray.

- Use the words, lines, or complete prayers in the offerings in the book.

- Acknowledge your distractions and that they're real.

- Excuse your distractions and let them know you'll return to them.

- Gently engage the practice in God's presence.

When You Pray

Pull music from every possible source and play it into me that the embers of persistence might churn and shift and renew me.

May those listening to the music being made in me sing.

Every word comes from you.

Ring words of wonder in me.

Let my depths be like melodies.

Let me become a chamber that reflects and echoes what you love.

Start in the quiet.

I want to discover music made there.

After You Pray

- Sit and listen.

- Write what you hear, sense, see.

- Create something.

- Keep praying.

- Write your own prayer.

WONDERING THROUGH THE MAZE

Before You Pray

- Choose a time to pray.

- Choose a place to pray.

- Use the words, lines, or complete prayers in the offerings in the book.

- Acknowledge your distractions and that they're real.

- Excuse your distractions and let them know you'll return to them.

- Gently engage the practice in God's presence.

When You Pray

My resolve to try is weak.

I am weak.

Turn me in so I can wonder through the maze of myself and find good words.

Turn me out so I can live full life and feed the bellies from which strengthening words come.

Seeing is impractical.

Make seeing so much a part of my days that I do it without thinking.

Grant that living and seeing and creating become synonyms so I can say in truth that I live well or write well or create well, and so that either statement identifies the other.

Spur me to focus on the important way of life, way of making, and way of creating.

It's hard to hear, see, and share what's within me.

It is often harder to attend to you.

The temptation to distraction is immeasurable.

Help me.

After You Pray

- Sit and listen.

- Write what you hear, sense, see.

- Create something.

- Keep praying.

- Write your own prayer.

IDEAS

Before You Pray

- Choose a time to pray.

- Choose a place to pray.

- Use the words, lines, or complete prayers in the offerings in the book.

- Acknowledge your distractions and that they're real.

- Excuse your distractions and let them know you'll return to them.

- Gently engage the practice in God's presence.

When You Pray

Countless ideas run around my head.

I find it hard to be centered in my noticing.

Sometimes my struggle is to start seeing anything at all.

Grant me the ability to see when my head is clouded, the ability to discern, the ability to hear when what's said is just beyond my ear's grasp.

I want the ability to put enough form to that thing that it feels.

Help me hold the idea gently.

Help me appreciate and respect the models you've given the world, the idea generators whose stories stay with me, whose ideas sustain my courage.

Help me hold things well, gently when needed and firmly when needed.

Loosen my hands in our quiet around those things you've invited me to release.

Tighten my heart around the things that make me love.

After You Pray

- Sit and listen.

- Write what you hear, sense, see.

- Create something.

- Keep praying.

- Write your own prayer.

SIFTING THROUGH THINGS

Before You Pray

- Choose a time to pray.

- Choose a place to pray.

- Use the words, lines, or complete prayers in the offerings in the book.

- Acknowledge your distractions and that they're real.

- Excuse your distractions and let them know you'll return to them.

- Gently engage the practice in God's presence.

When You Pray

Sift through the things, the mess and the garbage inside so that what I find is truly a treasure.

Pictures from years ago, trinkets broken by misuse or neglect, furniture that's no longer useful.

Search me and shine your light through so that I can see myself as a sparkling vessel capable of repeating the amazing in my work.

Prayers for Creativity

Enable me to organize, to structure, and to take one step after another.

Reclaim me.

Bless me.

Give me the gifts of something that can nourish the world.

May I use them for good.

Place in my heart strength and stamina so I can see those nourishing gifts on display.

And make me mindful to call them yours.

After You Pray

- Sit and listen.

- Write what you hear, sense, see.

- Create something.

- Keep praying.

- Write your own prayer.

OUTPOURING

Before You Pray

- Choose a time to pray.

- Choose a place to pray.

- Use the words, lines, or complete prayers in the offerings in the book.

- Acknowledge your distractions and that they're real.

- Excuse your distractions and let them know you'll return to them.

- Gently engage the practice in God's presence.

When You Pray

I've discarded boxes from my past.

I've left things I hoped to keep.

I've given away what I wanted to hold.

I've done what feels like a courageous thing.

Now, please, fill me.

Some of my soul places will remain empty.

Some of them are vessels for your use.

Pour into me.

Flow out of me.

For your good.

For the good of others.

After You Pray

- Sit and listen.

- Write what you hear, sense, see.

- Create something.

- Keep praying.

- Write your own prayer.

MY CLENCHED HANDS

Before You Pray

- Choose a time to pray.

- Choose a place to pray.

- Use the words, lines, or complete prayers in the offerings in the book.

- Acknowledge your distractions and that they're real.

- Excuse your distractions and let them know you'll return to them.

- Gently engage the practice in God's presence.

When You Pray

Hold my clenched hands.

Warm them as I try.

Keep your hands on mine.

Let me feel courage coming.

Prayers for Creativity

Clenching what I know restrains possibility.

Releasing my grip ends in my blessing.

I'm releasing my grip.

I'm in your hands.

After You Pray

- Sit and listen.

- Write what you hear, sense, see.

- Create something.

- Keep praying.

- Write your own prayer.

ONE SANCTUARY

Before You Pray

- Choose a time to pray.

- Choose a place to pray.

- Use the words, lines, or complete prayers in the offerings in the book.

- Acknowledge your distractions and that they're real.

- Excuse your distractions and let them know you'll return to them.

- Gently engage the practice in God's presence.

When You Pray

The air smells clean

Open my nose to your fragrance

Wide green stands and waves

Bless me with an open soul

A narrow path awaits

Encourage me to press forward

Others appear, coming and going

Inspire me by their steps

Shoes thumping, breath breathing, steady beating

Surround me in a song of praise

After You Pray

- Sit and listen.

- Write what you hear, sense, see.

- Create something.

- Keep praying.

- Write your own prayer.

UNSPEAKABLE

Before You Pray

- Choose a time to pray.

- Choose a place to pray.

- Use the words, lines, or complete prayers in the offerings in the book.

- Acknowledge your distractions and that they're real.

- Excuse your distractions and let them know you'll return to them.

- Gently engage the practice in God's presence.

When You Pray

My feet feel like dancing.

They express what my mouth can't.

My words fail me.

Rather than sit silent, I'll give my body room to do what I can't.

May my body expose the world to what you've given me.

May my body praise you in ways that words won't.

After You Pray

- Sit and listen.

- Write what you hear, sense, see.

- Create something.

- Keep praying.

- Write your own prayer.

GIVE ME JOY

Before You Pray

- Choose a time to pray.

- Choose a place to pray.

- Use the words, lines, or complete prayers in the offerings in the book.

- Acknowledge your distractions and that they're real.

- Excuse your distractions and let them know you'll return to them.

- Gently engage the practice in God's presence.

When You Pray

Narrow the long, wide fields of my world.

Identify my purposes as rooted in divine community.

Give me joy in doing less better and in, therefore, doing more.

Capture my mind with something sustainable, a character I can't forget or an act that returns again and again.

When my attention falters, gently bring me back.

When my energy wanes, lure me to return.

Help me continue looking, considering, telling, and doing all these with better language and increasing elegance and a large smile.

After You Pray

- Sit and listen.

- Write what you hear, sense, see.

- Create something.

- Keep praying.

- Write your own prayer.

COMMUNION WITH GOD

Before You Pray

- Choose a time to pray.

- Choose a place to pray.

- Use the words, lines, or complete prayers in the offerings in the book.

- Acknowledge your distractions and that they're real.

- Excuse your distractions and let them know you'll return to them.

- Gently engage the practice in God's presence.

When You Pray

In the silence, pull me into divine communion.

Take me in and show me what I need to see.

Show me who you are.

Show me who I am.

Show me a spiritual home.

Show me joy the way you've made it.

Joy is my destiny.

Joy is my future.

I'm headed for communion with God.

After You Pray

- Sit and listen.

- Write what you hear, sense, see.

- Create something.

- Keep praying.

- Write your own prayer.

THINGS I WONDER ABOUT

Before You Pray

- Choose a time to pray.

- Choose a place to pray.

- Use the words, lines, or complete prayers in the offerings in the book.

- Acknowledge your distractions and that they're real.

- Excuse your distractions and let them know you'll return to them.

- Gently engage the practice in God's presence.

When You Pray

Can this joy that I have be taken?

Can the bottom place of my soul be moved?

Can the eternal play that is my relationship to you be changed?

Hold my wonderings.

Host my questions.

Stretch me so that my questions open me to a new identity.

I am your child.

I am loved forever.

I am, from start to finish, in joy.

Help me to not wonder about that.

After You Pray

- Sit and listen.

- Write what you hear, sense, see.

- Create something.

- Keep praying.

- Write your own prayer.

MEMORY

Before You Pray

- Choose a time to pray.

- Choose a place to pray.

- Use the words, lines, or complete prayers in the offerings in the book.

- Acknowledge your distractions and that they're real.

- Excuse your distractions and let them know you'll return to them.

- Gently engage the practice in God's presence.

When You Pray

I won't always feel joy.

I may question the faint echo of it.

I may not sense happiness.

Or recognize goodness.

I may doubt they ever were.

When those things occur, give me the gift of memory.

Grant me grace to remember honestly.

Hold my memories open to my present.

Use my memories to minister to me.

After You Pray

- Sit and listen.

- Write what you hear, sense, see.

- Create something.

- Keep praying.

- Write your own prayer.

A WAY OPENING

Before You Pray

- Choose a time to pray.

- Choose a place to pray.

- Use the words, lines, or complete prayers in the offerings in the book.

- Acknowledge your distractions and that they're real.

- Excuse your distractions and let them know you'll return to them.

- Gently engage the practice in God's presence.

When You Pray

There is a way opening

And doors are also closing

I hear the sounds of change

I see the last times of this and that

My pace is slower in some ways

Prayers for Creativity

My heart quickens with beats of tomorrow

Off in that distance I'm smiling more

With the going of yesterday pains and its heart cracks

Comes my entrance into some spacious place

I'm sensing it, glimpsing it, smelling it, finally reaching
it

An imagination is emerging for the taste of those
meals

Feasts of bread taken up and wine slowly savored

Meals making me more me

After You Pray

- Sit and listen.

- Write what you hear, sense, see.

- Create something.

- Keep praying.

- Write your own prayer.

PRAYERS FOR DOUBT

"Hope accepts mystery and offers the gift of solid trust in the unknown. Hope doesn't pretend that I'll get all I want not does hope deny that there will still be struggles down the road. Hope tucks promises of growth and truth inside the pockets of my struggles."

Joyce Rupp, *Dear Heart, Come Home,* 141

UNKNOWING

Before You Pray

- Choose a time to pray.

- Choose a place to pray.

- Use the words, lines, or complete prayers in the offerings in the book.

- Acknowledge your distractions and that they're real.

- Excuse your distractions and let them know you'll return to them.

- Gently engage the practice in God's presence.

When You Pray

Unknowing shakes me.

The stress of the unseen turns me into a ball of questions, and I revel in answers.

Answers have been my security, knowing my guide.

You get this.

You understand me.

You know what it means to know all things.

You know the distance ahead of me as I make you my security and my strength.

Handle my unknowing and help me handle myself in the not knowing.

I want to see unknowing as the space where faith thrives.

After You Pray

- Sit and listen.

- Write what you hear, sense, see.

- Create something.

- Keep praying.

- Write your own prayer.

SWEET HOLY SPIRIT

Before You Pray

- Choose a time to pray.

- Choose a place to pray.

- Use the words, lines, or complete prayers in the offerings in the book.

- Acknowledge your distractions and that they're real.

- Excuse your distractions and let them know you'll return to them.

- Gently engage the practice in God's presence.

When You Pray

Mistrust cloaks me.

Sweet, holy spirit, overshadow me.

Pain frames my days.

Sweet, holy spirit, heal me.

Past sins sing.

Sweet, holy spirit, convince me.

Today frightens me.

Sweet, holy spirit, embolden me.

Anxieties swirl repeatedly.

Sweet, holy spirit, settle me.

Promises fail again.

Sweet, holy spirit, quicken me.

After You Pray

- Sit and listen.

- Write what you hear, sense, see.

- Create something.

- Keep praying.

- Write your own prayer.

IN YOUR HANDS

Before You Pray

- Choose a time to pray.

- Choose a place to pray.

- Use the words, lines, or complete prayers in the offerings in the book.

- Acknowledge your distractions and that they're real.

- Excuse your distractions and let them know you'll return to them.

- Gently engage the practice in God's presence.

When You Pray

My life has always been in your hands.

I'm disappointed at what feels like dismissals.

I thought this relationship would last.

I thought of an entire future.

I thought things would be enduring.

There's a deceptive voice in my ear.

It's telling me that my life has moved.

It's telling me that I'm not where I was.

Remind me today in the quiet that I'm in your hands.

After You Pray

- Sit and listen.

- Write what you hear, sense, see.

- Create something.

- Keep praying.

- Write your own prayer.

MY EYES

Before You Pray

- Choose a time to pray.

- Choose a place to pray.

- Use the words, lines, or complete prayers in the offerings in the book.

- Acknowledge your distractions and that they're real.

- Excuse your distractions and let them know you'll return to them.

- Gently engage the practice in God's presence.

When You Pray

Unfold faith in me when my hands clench doubt.

Pull the cord keeping me tied to what I see.

Spin me in twirling circles of hope.

Open my eyes.

Make my vision and visions clear, unencumbered by the litter of lifeless life.

Where I sit and, then, lay in faithlessness, give me confidence to rise.

Whisper the way babies do, in tones that are anything but quiet.

Call to what talent you've placed inside me.

After You Pray

- Sit and listen.

- Write what you hear, sense, see.

- Create something.

- Keep praying.

- Write your own prayer.

MY FUTURES

Before You Pray

- Choose a time to pray.

- Choose a place to pray.

- Use the words, lines, or complete prayers in the offerings in the book.

- Acknowledge your distractions and that they're real.

- Excuse your distractions and let them know you'll return to them.

- Gently engage the practice in God's presence.

When You Pray

Speak to my futures and talk until I believe enough to take one more step forward.

Grant the same loud whisper tomorrow and each following day.

When I'm overwhelmed, convince me to stay, to keep going, even when going is steep, hard, hardly possible.

Give me little bits of you even if I can't spot you, and make my day decorated with grace.

I will be lonely, and that loneliness will tempt me.

Please be more powerful than the emotion that comes from my long, bitter obedience.

Be more convincing than all the feelings within.

Be more.

After You Pray

- Sit and listen.

- Write what you hear, sense, see.

- Create something.

- Keep praying.

- Write your own prayer.

MY UNWRITTEN WORDS

Before You Pray

- Choose a time to pray.

- Choose a place to pray.

- Use the words, lines, or complete prayers in the offerings in the book.

- Acknowledge your distractions and that they're real.

- Excuse your distractions and let them know you'll return to them.

- Gently engage the practice in God's presence.

When You Pray

Unsaid words feel like burdens and still the sit on my tongue.

The feel just as heavy in my hands.

Waiting to be written, my words cram in the cracks of my fingers.

They are a symbol of all I have yet to do.

My unwritten words express my doubts.

I offer them to you, the smallest act of faith I can muster.

After You Pray

- Sit and listen.

- Write what you hear, sense, see.

- Create something.

- Keep praying.

- Write your own prayer.

WIDE INVITATIONS

Before You Pray

- Choose a time to pray.

- Choose a place to pray.

- Use the words, lines, or complete prayers in the offerings in the book.

- Acknowledge your distractions and that they're real.

- Excuse your distractions and let them know you'll return to them.

- Gently engage the practice in God's presence.

When You Pray

Enable me to see the blank page as a gift and a friend.

Brighten the background of the empty page

Until it becomes a wide invitation.

Creator of the best stories,

Maker of the most enduring truths about humanity,

Answer my prayers.

After You Pray

- Sit and listen.

- Write what you hear, sense, see.

- Create something.

- Keep praying.

- Write your own prayer.

FISTS AND FINGERS

Before You Pray

- Choose a time to pray.

- Choose a place to pray.

- Use the words, lines, or complete prayers in the offerings in the book.

- Acknowledge your distractions and that they're real.

- Excuse your distractions and let them know you'll return to them.

- Gently engage the practice in God's presence.

When You Pray

See the page as I see it.

See the unasked question, the untaken risk, and the small possibility as I do.

Notice my fears, most of which I keep inside.

Count my hopes and measure the distance between what I want and what I'm able to accomplish.

I feel my faith stretching out from the ground of my being.

Sometimes the faith feels strong like a fist pressed high in the sky.

Sometimes faith feels like a finger, weak and bent and alone.

After You Pray

- Sit and listen.

- Write what you hear, sense, see.

- Create something.

- Keep praying.

- Write your own prayer.

JOIN ME

Before You Pray

- Choose a time to pray.

- Choose a place to pray.

- Use the words, lines, or complete prayers in the offerings in the book.

- Acknowledge your distractions and that they're real.

- Excuse your distractions and let them know you'll return to them.

- Gently engage the practice in God's presence.

When You Pray

Join me in the quiet aloneness.

Feel weak with me or strong with me.

In your seeing things as I do, grant me new vision to see the unimaginable.

Make what I can't see imaginable.

After You Pray

- Sit and listen.

- Write what you hear, sense, see.

- Create something.

- Keep praying.

- Write your own prayer.

SKILLS OF GRATITUDE

Before You Pray

- Choose a time to pray.

- Choose a place to pray.

- Use the words, lines, or complete prayers in the offerings in the book.

- Acknowledge your distractions and that they're real.

- Excuse your distractions and let them know you'll return to them.

- Gently engage the practice in God's presence.

When You Pray

Give me the skills of gratitude.

Form me into a thankful writer, grateful for language and its gifts.

Make me fearless as one page ends.

Grant that I might see you in the blankness of what's next.

Press into me faith and imagination because writing requires both.

And may I, in some way, offer you all I do.

And may my offerings entertain you, the most perceptive and faithful Reader.

After You Pray

- Sit and listen.

- Write what you hear, sense, see.

- Create something.

- Keep praying.

- Write your own prayer.

RISK

Before You Pray

- Choose a time to pray.

- Choose a place to pray.

- Use the words, lines, or complete prayers in the offerings in the book.

- Acknowledge your distractions and that they're real.

- Excuse your distractions and let them know you'll return to them.

- Gently engage the practice in God's presence.

When You Pray

Track the meanings of all the unwritten words

Make sense, especially when I can't, of why writing and living and trying and risking matter.

Make me unafraid of the page.

Help me to imagine my creation full and crowded.

Excite me over tomorrow.

When today's phrases have felt forced,

When this day's work is tired,

Because I tried and wrote but didn't finish.

Risk with me.

After You Pray

- Sit and listen.

- Write what you hear, sense, see.

- Create something.

- Keep praying.

- Write your own prayer.

ENDURING THE BROADNESS

Before You Pray

- Choose a time to pray.

- Choose a place to pray.

- Use the words, lines, or complete prayers in the offerings in the book.

- Acknowledge your distractions and that they're real.

- Excuse your distractions and let them know you'll return to them.

- Gently engage the practice in God's presence.

When You Pray

Endure the broadness of my unanswered questions. Endure the broadness of occasional doubts, hard-uttered gratitude, resentment, wondering, knowing and not knowing, and waiting. Bless my efforts to restore myself and where I fall short, close the gaps.

Make me laugh because doubt troubles my joy. Make me sit and stir and run in joy because I've so long separated doubt from faith as if they aren't essentially connected. Fill my day with splendid memories from times when I have believed. Make memory a gift to my future. Open before me a fullness of faith, a changed faith, one that owns and claims the broadness as its own.

After You Pray

- Sit and listen.

- Write what you hear, sense, see.

- Create something.

- Keep praying.

- Write your own prayer.

PRAYERS FOR GRIEF

"Every great loss demands that we choose life again. We need to grieve in order to do this. The pain we have not grieved over will always stand between us and life…Grieving is not about forgetting. Grieving allows us to heal, to remember with love rather than pain. It is a sorting process."

Rachel Noemi Remen, *My Grandfather's Blessings*, 38

NOTICING LOSSES

Before You Pray

- Choose a time to pray.

- Choose a place to pray.

- Use the words, lines, or complete prayers in the offerings in the book.

- Acknowledge your distractions and that they're real.

- Excuse your distractions and let them know you'll return to them.

- Gently engage the practice in God's presence.

When You Pray

My losses are real.

So are my loves.

I won't turn away from either.

I will face my loves in the company of God.

I will notice my losses there, too.

I am weakened when I lose but only because I'm learning to love.

I am bruised by loss and wrecked by grief but I am a better lover.

I've noticed my loss.

I will notice my love.

I will notice your love.

After You Pray

- Sit and listen.

- Write what you hear, sense, see.

- Create something.

- Keep praying.

- Write your own prayer.

DADDY

Before You Pray

- Choose a time to pray.

- Choose a place to pray.

- Use the words, lines, or complete prayers in the offerings in the book.

- Acknowledge your distractions and that they're real.

- Excuse your distractions and let them know you'll return to them.

- Gently engage the practice in God's presence.

When You Pray

I miss him.

In whatever way you can, tell him.

I love him.

In whatever way you can, show him.

After You Pray

- Sit and listen.

- Write what you hear, sense, see.

- Create something.

- Keep praying.

- Write your own prayer.

ACQUAINTED WITH GRIEF

Before You Pray

- Choose a time to pray.

- Choose a place to pray.

- Use the words, lines, or complete prayers in the offerings in the book.

- Acknowledge your distractions and that they're real.

- Excuse your distractions and let them know you'll return to them.

- Gently engage the practice in God's presence.

When You Pray

You are acquainted with grief.

What do you know that you can teach me?

You are acquainted with grief.

What have you embodied that mirrors my insides?

You are acquainted with grief.

How were you changed and how will I be?

You are acquainted with grief.

When will my heart enlarge to love the way you love?

You are acquainted with grief.

After You Pray

- Sit and listen.

- Write what you hear, sense, see.

- Create something.

- Keep praying.

- Write your own prayer.

ROOMS FOR MY GRIEF

Before You Pray

- Choose a time to pray.

- Choose a place to pray.

- Use the words, lines, or complete prayers in the offerings in the book.

- Acknowledge your distractions and that they're real.

- Excuse your distractions and let them know you'll return to them.

- Gently engage the practice in God's presence.

When You Pray

My grief needs its own room.

Each loss needs a place, a home.

Even if for a short stay, my pain needs a host.

Join me in drawing the plans, sketching the interior for these parts of me.

Help me respect my hard losses and the soft grief each brings.

Let's create rooms to hold this pain, to honor this hurt, and to heal.

Give me courage to rest in those rooms.

Give me eyes to see you settling there.

Give me acceptance of what you bring when you come.

After You Pray

- Sit and listen.

- Write what you hear, sense, see.

- Create something.

- Keep praying.

- Write your own prayer.

PRESSING ME AWAY

Before You Pray

- Choose a time to pray.

- Choose a place to pray.

- Use the words, lines, or complete prayers in the offerings in the book.

- Acknowledge your distractions and that they're real.

- Excuse your distractions and let them know you'll return to them.

- Gently engage the practice in God's presence.

When You Pray

Grief makes me question whether you've gone.

Loads of sorrows press me away.

I know you're there.

I even sense you.

Still, those traumas crowd out scenes of grace.

Grace couldn't be in all the dark before me.

You couldn't be in those hellish moments.

Or could you?

After You Pray

- Sit and listen.

- Write what you hear, sense, see.

- Create something.

- Keep praying.

- Write your own prayer.

QUESTIONS

Before You Pray

- Choose a time to pray.

- Choose a place to pray.

- Use the words, lines, or complete prayers in the offerings in the book.

- Acknowledge your distractions and that they're real.

- Excuse your distractions and let them know you'll return to them.

- Gently engage the practice in God's presence.

When You Pray

Perhaps Lucy's question emerges for grace-filled reasons

Those questions frame any visit from God

Questions spill on the floor like blood in a trauma bay

What's the grace you need?

Who's the God you need?

How is the Spirit present?

What is God doing?

How are you?

After You Pray

- Sit and listen.

- Write what you hear, sense, see.

- Create something.

- Keep praying.

- Write your own prayer.

TEARS

Before You Pray

- Choose a time to pray.

- Choose a place to pray.

- Use the words, lines, or complete prayers in the offerings in the book.

- Acknowledge your distractions and that they're real.

- Excuse your distractions and let them know you'll return to them.

- Gently engage the practice in God's presence.

When You Pray

Teach me the meaning of those tears.

The tears down my face and down the faces of others.

Tell me the story of those tears.

The tears I've wiped away, the ones that have dried.

Deepen my acquaintance with pain.

The pains that hide in my soul, the hurts darkened by time.

Count those experiences in lovely tones

And make me able to hear your kind voice.

After You Pray

- Sit and listen.

- Write what you hear, sense, see.

- Create something.

- Keep praying.

- Write your own prayer.

LYNCHING

Before You Pray

- Choose a time to pray.

- Choose a place to pray.

- Use the words, lines, or complete prayers in the offerings in the book.

- Acknowledge your distractions and that they're real.

- Excuse your distractions and let them know you'll return to them.

- Gently engage the practice in God's presence.

When You Pray

How long will you watch these same scenes?

Don't you care the way our bodies are displayed across pages and screens?

Hasn't the blood trickled from every direction and stopped at you?

Who is this prayer for, me or you?

Am I doing enough?

I look at my hands and my feet?

Have I fought hard?

Does the Divine question this way?

Does God ask questions the way I am?

What do you say?

After You Pray

- Sit and listen.

- Write what you hear, sense, see.

- Create something.

- Keep praying.

- Write your own prayer.

SHEDDING AND GAINING

Before You Pray

- Choose a time to pray.

- Choose a place to pray.

- Use the words, lines, or complete prayers in the offerings in the book.

- Acknowledge your distractions and that they're real.

- Excuse your distractions and let them know you'll return to them.

- Gently engage the practice in God's presence.

When You Pray

Shedding of blood

Shedding of tears

Shedding of innocence

Shedding of pride

Shedding of assurance

Shedding of fixes

Shedding of answers

Shedding of gods

Shedding of me

Gaining love

After You Pray

- Sit and listen.

- Write what you hear, sense, see.

- Create something.

- Keep praying.

- Write your own prayer.

ON A HILL

Before You Pray

- Choose a time to pray.

- Choose a place to pray.

- Use the words, lines, or complete prayers in the offerings in the book.

- Acknowledge your distractions and that they're real.

- Excuse your distractions and let them know you'll return to them.

- Gently engage the practice in God's presence.

When You Pray

Scratches in my throat remind me of my screams.

They remind me that I can't drink.

There's no pleasure in favorite beverages.

My mouth is irritated by all that talking, all that processing.

I've listened to myself and I sound furious.

In therapy, I sound thirsty.

In prayer, I am desperate.

I'm sitting on the faraway hill.

My knees are buckling under the weight.

I was standing but I'm too weak to do that.

Dryness is my companion.

After You Pray

- Sit and listen.

- Write what you hear, sense, see.

- Create something.

- Keep praying.

- Write your own prayer.

TRUST

Before You Pray

- Choose a time to pray.

- Choose a place to pray.

- Use the words, lines, or complete prayers in the offerings in the book.

- Acknowledge your distractions and that they're real.

- Excuse your distractions and let them know you'll return to them.

- Gently engage the practice in God's presence.

When You Pray

Someone I trust told me you'd come.

I'm still waiting for you to be who you've been to me.

Now, of course, I know that you've come and gone and come again.

But you're not the same as before.

Each time you've come, you've been faithful.

But you've been different.

Different in that new way that I'm only open to after the losses.

I trust you.

I can't tell what healing you'll bring.

I know that I'll never have what has passed through my hands.

But I will have me and I will have you.

And I will have love.

Trust will return in some form.

After You Pray

- Sit and listen.

- Write what you hear, sense, see.

- Create something.

- Keep praying.

- Write your own prayer.

PRAYERS FOR OTHERS

As a human being, then, he belongs to life and the whole kingdom of life that includes all that lives and perhaps, also, all that has ever lived. In other words, he sees himself as a part of a continuing, breathing, living existence. To be a human being, then, is to be essentially alive in a living world."

Howard Thurman, *The Luminous Darkness*, 94

PRAYERS OF THE PEOPLE

Before You Pray

- Choose a time to pray.

- Choose a place to pray.

- Use the words, lines, or complete prayers in the offerings in the book.

- Acknowledge your distractions and that they're real.

- Excuse your distractions and let them know you'll return to them.

- Gently engage the practice in God's presence.

When You Pray

It's bruising to pray well, to talk to you during these trials.

It's hard to pray honestly, to open to you during all these parades of white supremacy.

It's hard because I have to pray about bald-faced evil terrorizing us.

It's one thing to pray for the long-stretched out problems.

It's another to pray for things that God has left for me to do, for us to do.

It's an altogether other thing to pray for things that turn God's eyes.

In these moments of quiet, grant me the grace to pray for hard things.

Place before me the people and situations that I need to hold up to you.

After You Pray

- Sit and listen.

- Write what you hear, sense, see.

- Create something.

- Keep praying.

- Write your own prayer.

WHAT I CAN'T FACE

Before You Pray

- Choose a time to pray.

- Choose a place to pray.

- Use the words, lines, or complete prayers in the offerings in the book.

- Acknowledge your distractions and that they're real.

- Excuse your distractions and let them know you'll return to them.

- Gently engage the practice in God's presence.

When You Pray

It's hard talking to you the way I once did.

It's hard doing anything the way I once did.

I can't ignore things that are hard to face.

I can't stay busy enough so that I keep avoiding the unavoidable parts of my life.

Give me strength to face what I can't face.

Stay beside me when I see what's there.

After You Pray

- Sit and listen.

- Write what you hear, sense, see.

- Create something.

- Keep praying.

- Write your own prayer.

YOUR JOB

Before You Pray

- Choose a time to pray.

- Choose a place to pray.

- Use the words, lines, or complete prayers in the offerings in the book.

- Acknowledge your distractions and that they're real.

- Excuse your distractions and let them know you'll return to them.

- Gently engage the practice in God's presence.

When You Pray

Help me trust you and not fear.

Help me pick up, notice, and pay attention to the things on the floor inside me.

Help me stand and see what I want to avoid.

When life is messy and crowded, make sure that I know you're there.

That's your job, not mine.

I can't make myself feel you.

Come close to me and love me and never let me forget that I'm yours.

After You Pray

- Sit and listen.

- Write what you hear, sense, see.

- Create something.

- Keep praying.

- Write your own prayer.

LOVED

Before You Pray

- Choose a time to pray.

- Choose a place to pray.

- Use the words, lines, or complete prayers in the offerings in the book.

- Acknowledge your distractions and that they're real.

- Excuse your distractions and let them know you'll return to them.

- Gently engage the practice in God's presence.

When You Pray

You love me without condition.

I will rest under that weight.

Be blanketed in it.

Held by it.

I am loved.

God loves me.

After You Pray

- Sit and listen.

- Write what you hear, sense, see.

- Create something.

- Keep praying.

- Write your own prayer.

FOR A FRIEND WHO'S HOSPITALIZED

Before You Pray

- Choose a time to pray.

- Choose a place to pray.

- Use the words, lines, or complete prayers in the offerings in the book.

- Acknowledge your distractions and that they're real.

- Excuse your distractions and let them know you'll return to them.

- Gently engage the practice in God's presence.

When You Pray

You are more than enough.

You are a company-keeper.

You are a God who heals.

You are the one working through every touch.

You are aware of what's next.

Grant patience when everything takes too long.

Grant guidance when questions scream and answers don't.

Grant awareness when the darkness unfolds in uncertainty.

Grant resilience when resolve and hope hide.

You are more than enough.

You are a company-keeper.

You are a God who heals.

You are the one working through every touch.

You are aware of what's next.

After You Pray

- Sit and listen.

- Write what you hear, sense, see.

- Create something.

- Keep praying.

- Write your own prayer.

FOR A FRIEND LOOKING FOR WORK

Before You Pray

- Choose a time to pray.

- Choose a place to pray.

- Use the words, lines, or complete prayers in the offerings in the book.

- Acknowledge your distractions and that they're real.

- Excuse your distractions and let them know you'll return to them.

- Gently engage the practice in God's presence.

When You Pray

Center him in his identity.

Who he is comes from you.

What he does matters.

What he does doesn't matter.

You want to use him.

You love him if he doesn't get used.

You love him.

Keep loving him.

After You Pray

- Sit and listen.

- Write what you hear, sense, see.

- Create something.

- Keep praying.

- Write your own prayer.

FOR STUDENTS AND TEACHERS BEGINNING

Before You Pray

- Choose a time to pray.

- Choose a place to pray.

- Use the words, lines, or complete prayers in the offerings in the book.

- Acknowledge your distractions and that they're real.

- Excuse your distractions and let them know you'll return to them.

- Gently engage the practice in God's presence.

When You Pray

As we start, we give you our objectives and hopes, mentioned and unmentioned.

We offer all our preparation, all the meetings and every act that brought us to this point.

Thank you for each person who has given something to this course, to our studies, to our growth.

Grant that we might meet each other, and in meeting each other, meet you.

In our reading, rushed or patient.

In our writing and reflection.

In every act and endeavor.

Be around the edges and in the center.

Be pleased and bless us with your company.

Calm our fears.

Be more than enough as we meet one another.

Teach us to listen.

Show us – in the doing, reading, and attending – yourself.

Teach us in our studies to pray.

After You Pray

- Sit and listen.

- Write what you hear, sense, see.

- Create something.

- Keep praying.

- Write your own prayer.

A FRIEND STRUGGLING WITH SUICIDAL THOUGHTS

Before You Pray

- Choose a time to pray.

- Choose a place to pray.

- Use the words, lines, or complete prayers in the offerings in the book.

- Acknowledge your distractions and that they're real.

- Excuse your distractions and let them know you'll return to them.

- Gently engage the practice in God's presence.

When You Pray

You know that pain, the depth of it.

Fall as far down as possible.

Lean into the experience of my friend.

Before my love is your love.

Continue that love.

Hold that pain.

Lessen that weight.

Bring healing.

Bring hope.

Bring healing.

Be loving.

After You Pray

- Sit and listen.

- Write what you hear, sense, see.

- Create something.

- Keep praying.

- Write your own prayer.

FOR A FRIEND READYING FOR MARRIAGE

Before You Pray

- Choose a time to pray.

- Choose a place to pray.

- Use the words, lines, or complete prayers in the offerings in the book.

- Acknowledge your distractions and that they're real.

- Excuse your distractions and let them know you'll return to them.

- Gently engage the practice in God's presence.

When You Pray

As he anticipates his vows, anchor him in truth.

Truth is what's present and real and perfect.

He needs to know who you've made him to be.

How he's loved.

How he's made.

How his constitution is full of grace given by you.

Many things matter with marriage.

Love matters first.

Love matters last.

As she readies for her pledge, deepen her conviction to reality.

Reality is what's true and real and perfect.

Make her aware of whom she is in you.

How she's loved.

How she's made.

How her constitution is full of grace given by you.

Many things matter with marriage.

Love matters first.

Love matters last.

AFTER YOU PRAY

1. Sit and listen. Prayer goes in more than one direction. It is communication between you and God, between you and God. Listen for what God might "say," even if that message isn't heard in an audible way. It probably won't be, which makes it more interesting!

2. Write what you hear, sense, see. Taking note of what the Spirit offers builds your intimacy with God because it shows that what God gives matters to you. Hold onto it by writing it down. You might return to it. You might need it later.

3. Draw a picture. Create something. If it's not a picture, make something else to employ a part of your mind. Centering prayer opens the soul and the spirit. Using another creative part of yourself may help you come to the next moment.

4. Keep praying. To the extent that prayer is a conversation with God, prayer is happening when you speak to or hear from God, and prayer is happening when God does the same. Find a way to keep praying, however you conceptualize it. Keep centering.

5. Write your own prayer. I've given you ways and words to pray, and I've done so in order to prime you for the same activity. Perhaps you can write one-sentence each day.

About Michael K. Washington

Michael is a chaplain and pastoral educator at Northwestern Memorial Hospital. He is an ordained Covenant pastor and served two different congregations for a total of sixteen years up until the fall of 2017 when he transitioned to only working in one pastoral context. Occasionally, he teaches as an adjunct in an area seminary or leads retreats in his areas of interest. Michael's education includes the conversations he has with family, mentors, friends, and a great spiritual director. It also includes courses of study at the University of Illinois at Urbana-Champaign where he completed a BS in psychology, Wheaton College where he completed a MA in theology, and Garrett-Evangelical Theological Seminary where he completed a MDiv. Michael recently began doctoral study in pastoral theology, personality, and culture at GETS and it will be among his latest growth experiences.

www.ingramcontent.com/pod-product-compliance
Lightning Source LLC
Chambersburg PA
CBHW051820040426
42447CB00006B/297